Off to the Right Start

Illustrations by **ALIDA MARSH**
Sketch-studies by **WILLIAM JAEGER**

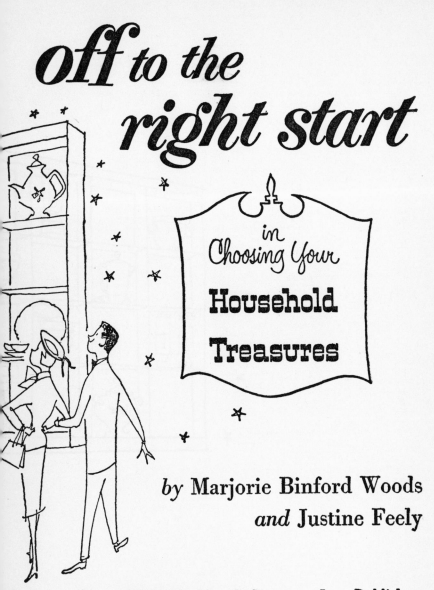

off to the right start

right start

in Choosing Your Household Treasures

by **Marjorie Binford Woods**
and **Justine Feely**

The Bobbs-Merrill Company, Inc., *Publishers*
INDIANAPOLIS · NEW YORK

First Edition

Dedicated to You-Two
and your thrilling adventures
into treasure land.
May you have home-harmony
and happiness
right from the start!

TABLE OF CONTENTS

TABLE OF CONTENTS

Chapter III

SELECTING YOUR SILVER

38-63

CHAPTER IV
YOUR GLASSWARE
64-89

CHAPTER V
YOUR LINENS
90-133

TABLE OF CONTENTS

CHAPTER VI

MECHANICAL HELPERS

134-173

CHAPTER VII

KITCHEN NECESSITIES

174-187

TABLE OF CONTENTS

CHAPTER VIII

PUTTING YOUR TREASURES TO WORK

189-229

SKETCH STUDIES

Off to the Right Start

CHAPTER I

WHAT IS THE RIGHT START?

THIS IS A BOOK ESPECIALLY DESIGNED TO HELP YOU AND YOUR man fall in love with your home just as you fell in love with each other. True compatibility is the keynote of your happiness together, and likewise should be the keynote for everything you choose to live with.

It takes much more than a collection of household items to make a real home, to be sure. But as a starting point it's logical to turn your attention to the small (but important) household treasures that are to set the tone of your day-by-day life together.

High on this line-up of accessories are those ever-lovin' mechanical aids that save you time and energy; the selection of handsome china, silver and glassware for your table, pretty linens for bedroom and bath—all the charming accouterments that reveal your own individuality and make your fireside a glowing place where family and friends love to gather.

Never before in your experience has any selection of purchases scored such a sky-high rating in your book of buymanship as these small coin-of-marriage possessions now assume. Along with the option on your third finger, left hand, will come a new code of values, an added aura of satisfaction in sharing, and a greater measure of pride in ownership.

Many of the things you invest in now will become more beautiful and more valuable as the years go by. So whether it's a silver spoon, a satin coverlet or a shimmering crystal goblet which you are considering as a household companion, you'll want to weigh your decisions well, get *his* nod of approval, then make certain before you sign up for each piece that it promises to be love for keeps and a joy forever.

dream to a definite plan

The way your new home looks will depend on your taste and ideas, not merely on the dollars that you put into it. Naturally you will need some down-to-earth principles to go by and a heap o' learnin' to guide you in your choices, if you are one who has never had any experience or practical training in how to go about setting up the makings of a home.

You'll want to dream to a plan that not only brings happy living to your very first home but that looks ahead to unfoldment and expansion in your good fortune together—a plan that makes even casual living a real art because of the understanding you have in knowing how to carry it out to perfection.

Since it's up to you to cope with both dreams and practical realities at the same time, begin now by letting this book be your compass and lodestar to lead you along your happy way.

To get the most out of its pages, follow the shopping guidelines and information charts, making notes as you go in your household plan book. Heed the lists of requirements for your type of living and help yourself to the quick-to-pick-up addenda on just what you need to know.

While friends and relatives are busy telling you what *they* think you ought to have, you-two can be smart and steal a march on them by boning up on the right answers and asserting *your own* prerogatives.

Hand in hand with information contained in this book
you'll also need
1. a good measure of common sense
2. an eagerness to learn
3. a spirit of adventure and enjoyment
4. a sharing attitude
5. individual imagination
6. money to spend but none to waste

formula for gilt-edged investing

Young bank rolls are usually somewhat limited, but even so, you'll doubtless have a certain sum figured out that you can afford to spend on the "first loves" of your home.

Beauty is not necessarily inherent in a price tag. Nor is harmony in the associated accessories you buy dependent on their relative prices.

Good things may seem to be expensive, however. And, since

the very wisest rule for buying is to invest in the best quality you can possibly afford, you may perforce start out with fewer pieces than you originally planned, then add to them as you can.

It will pay you to put your money into fine workmanship and materials that will be a constant source of pride through the many years to come. So don't be rushed into buying make-shift things, or "special bargains," as a compromise.

Shop only in the most reliable stores for your purchases of value. Don't for a minute minimize the quality and the guarantee that backs up quality.

Seek out the famous brand names and nationally known manufacturers for your investments, and put yourself in the hands of a counselor in the Wedding Gift Registry department of your favorite store for budget information and all-round good advice. Whatever your status, whether bride-to-be, bride, or gift purchaser, you are always a welcome guest in the gift departments—to look, to check and to counsel to your heart's content.

What if it is a shoestring start? It's love, isn't it?

make your choices by rule of heart

Since the climate or atmosphere of your home will be determined more or less by your choice of accessories, it is important to know your leanings in the way of design, color and style before you go foraging into the unknown.

Will you and your bridegroom be happiest in a colorful and casual background . . . would you prefer quiet elegance . . . or something daringly urban? Should the décor be modern in tone, traditional, Early American, or French Provincial?

Answers to these questions will give you an inkling, at least, as to what types of appointments will be most adaptable to your mode of living. And to start your formulating your own ideas, why not make up a scrapbook of color schemes, table settings and home accessories from magazine tear sheets and clippings? Then hold a series of sessions with your rangier half to talk over what you like and what you don't like, making note of favored colors, styles and designs.

These first choices of yours, if completely compatible to you both, can serve as a real cue toward your home decorating scheme later on. And instead of matching the trimmings of your house to the major furnishings, reverse the usual method and let your china, or crystal, silver, or linen be the source of inspiration for the color and style of your rooms.

In exchanging ideas with your friends on prospective patterns don't let yourselves be unduly influenced by what others in your crowd are selecting, or by what Cousin Jane prefers.

Your job, as a wise and witty wife, is to take the lead in planning a home that will reflect the two of you and be an ever-renewing source of enjoyment, inspiration and peace. The recommended way to lay the groundwork is to view everything you desire through a double-vision lens, then make your choices by rule of heart, as well as by rule of head.

your role as hostess

This new role of hostess is not something that can be created by you alone but by the togetherness you share with your husband, by your more meaningful way of life, the security of a newly established home and the glow of happiness.

Your attitude toward homemaking will pretty well determine your aptitude. You are a *natural* for it

if—your interest and planning go deeper than a mere "lick and promise."

if—you have a keen knowledge and appreciation of the flick-of-the-switch equipment you need in a twentieth-century house.

if—you can be as charming and gracious a hostess to your husband day by day as you are when you are entertaining guests.

Your talents will pay off in big dividends if you equip and run your house easily, airily, comfortably—and do it with a flair. Even the most casual way of living, however, follows certain accepted codes and conventions in carrying out the amenities of hospitality, and knowing the rules gives you more assurance for deliberately breaking them, when you dare to.

That's why the sooner you make yourselves "at home" with your new possessions and learn how to get the most out of them, the sooner you'll be proving yourself a genius in woman's most important job—that of being a wife, hostess and helpmate.

CHAPTER II

CHOOSING YOUR CHINA

HERE'S WHERE THE REAL FUN BEGINS.

Your dreaming days are over and the *doing days* are here.

Soon you'll have the opportunity of expressing in reality all the thoughts and plans you've been nursing along during your growing-up years.

19

"When I get married, I'm going to have beautiful blue Wedgwood china just like Aunt Ann's." That's what you always used to say.

But now you may have different ideas. You realize that it's not entirely *your* decision any more. And you're happy that it isn't, that there is a *somebody special* to consider and consult.

There is much to learn about these treasures of beauty for which you are soon to be searching. But what a world of satisfaction and enjoyment is to be had in gathering this knowledge as you go along from plates to appliances, from linens to ladles. Already you're aware that this new role of homemaker can be as big as your own imagination, and twice as much fun as anything you've ever known before.

We're suggesting that you start your table-setting co-ordination with china as your keynote. But there is no rule which says that china should be selected first. It may very well be silver which will demand your initial attention, if you prefer it that way.

But whatever your order of plan and purchase, the principal point is that you should make a background study of the specific items in which you are interested before you go out to shop. Learn all you can about the general subject, so that you can judge individual pieces with authority when you find them, and can appreciate their fine points.

After you have read each chapter in this book (starting right here with china) do some good, concentrated thinking about your needs and wants from a realistic viewpoint. Figure out what you naturally like best, what will serve you best, and what you can best afford.

Then when it comes time to make your final selections you can judge with intelligence and some measure of surety. Only in this way will you feel competent and free to express your own taste and individuality in lasting choices.

what does the word "china" mean to you?

It may mean the memory of grandmother's treasured Lowestoft teapot, or your own little rose-sprigged dishes that you played with as a child. Whatever it recalls, you undoubtedly have acquired a love and respect for beautiful china and a desire to possess it.

Like other worth-while achievements, fine china was developed over a long period of time by men who devoted their lives to searching for a formula combining beauty and durability.

It all started 'way back about the sixth century when the Chinese produced a very fine translucent porcelain. As the brave traders began rounding the Cape of Good Hope along about the sixteenth century, they brought back pieces of this porcelain to the Continent. In England it was called Chinaware since it came from China, but this was soon shortened to the common noun, "china."

For over two hundred years many attempts were made to copy this exquisite ware, but it wasn't until early in the eighteenth century that an alchemist, John Boettger of Dresden, decided to try the white powder he used on his wig. This was it. The powder contained the fine white clay which is the basic material of porcelain.

A royal pottery was established at Meissen, Germany,

famous source of Dresden china. Within a few years England was making use of the secret, as was France, and in the nineteenth century beautiful china was first made in America by Walter Scott Lenox.

formerly for the favored few

During that early period only persons of great wealth could afford fine china. Kings and queens ordered special services that cost thousands of dollars. But the skillful modern production methods now make it possible for practically everyone to own good china.

These modern production methods do not mean mass production, however. Fine china is still handmade. Skilled hands continue to press the clay into molds, to trim and finish each single piece with dexterity. One teacup may require the skill of seventy different handcraftmen before it is finished. So when it reaches you, each piece of fine china is a true work of art, something to be treasured.

is all china "real" china?

Briefly that is the story of fine china. The term now is used almost generically, however, to designate every type of dinnerware. Stores have their "china" sections, which include everything from a crude pottery bowl to the most expensive gold-encrusted china plate.

All "china" is "ceramic," which means it is made of clay and baked, but there are wide differences which you will recognize when shopping. There are two classifications of so-called "china."

Earthenware: This kind is thicker and more porous; it has a tendency to crack. It is opaque, no light appears through it. *Pottery,* the cheapest kind of earthenware, is heaviest and most breakable of all.

Fine china: This kind is porcelain, made of fine clays and fired at a higher heat than earthenware, which gives it more strength, though it looks more fragile. *Bone china* is a type of fine china which contains a mixture of bone ash that gives it a characteristic whiteness. This is found only in English china.

Semivitreous or *semiporcelain* may be terms which you will hear in connection with china, but don't be confused. Semi-vitreous ware is *not* china but has a harder body than earthenware. It has no translucence and no ringing sound. English dinnerware of the semivitreous type is called "fine earthenware."

how to test

Here's a quick test for determining the difference between earthenware and china. Hold a piece of china to the light. It is translucent and you'll see your fingers silhouetted through it. It also has a bell-like ring if struck with a pencil or one's fingernail.

Earthenware has no translucence, and makes a dull, heavy sound when tapped with a pencil. Just for illustration, if you ever have the opportunity to test a piece of fine china that has been broken, you'll find that the china will not absorb

water or grease, even though the glaze is chipped. Earthenware, on the other hand, is of porous body and reacts much
like blotting paper.

introducing decoration

There are two types of decoration used on china and earthenware, and the decorating process employed on both is much
the same.

Underglaze: The pattern has been put on the body before the
glaze has been baked on. This makes the decoration
very durable.

Overglaze: The designs are applied to the surface of the finishing glaze; the ware is placed in the kiln, or oven,
and the colors are fused with the glaze at a moderate
temperature.

Underglaze decoration will withstand unlimited use without changing in color or texture, and will not wash off. Of
the two glazes it is the more permanent one.

Overglaze decorations, however, are more popular because
of the wide range of colors possible in this process of surface
finishing.

what determines price?

Since earthenware is simpler to produce, it costs less. Its

quality and price depend, however, on the care which the manufacturer uses in making and decorating it.

Some fine earthenware is as expensive as plain china. On the other hand, earthenware also comes in a wide range of inexpensive patterns and styles.

Earthenware lends itself naturally to bright, intense colors, since it doesn't have to be fired at such high temperatures. Sometimes the body itself is tinted, and colored glazes are used, just as are the transparent ones.

Decoration determines the price of *all* dinnerware.

1. Patterns may be hand-painted, which is the most expensive process.

2. Printed by decalcomania, which is cheapest of all.

3. Printed in outline form and filled in by hand. (In this you pay for each brush stroke of the artist.)

There are two kinds of gold decoration: coin gold and luster gold. Coin gold is pure gold which is burnished or rubbed to a soft sheen. Luster is a liquid prepared with a small amount of gold, which produces a bright golden surface. This is considerably less in price than coin gold.

Etched gold designs are used on large service plates and costly dinnerware. A design is etched in the glaze with acid, and coin gold is applied to the etched portion. After burnishing, the high parts of the etched design stand out against the duller background. This is sometimes called "encrusted gold."

is imported china best?

Many may have the mistaken idea that all the really good

china comes from abroad. (It's probably a holdover from Grandmother's day.)

Of course, imported china is lovely and durable, and if you find a pattern you favor among the various designs, by all means select it.

Remember, however, that there are any number of American names which stand for the same beauty and quality that you find in the imports. Outstanding contributions have been made by American dinnerware manufacturers in excellent glazes that are almost as hard as steel, in daring shapes and original forms, and in colors of every hue.

what suits you?

What type of life do you plan to lead in that first home of yours? Will you start out in an efficiency apartment, a bedroom apartment, or a house in the suburbs? Will you entertain much?

All these factors enter into the selection of the kind and the amount of dinnerware you will choose.

Then there's the question of the *type* (or period) of furnishings you're planning to buy. Even in a so-called furnished apartment, you'll want to start collecting your own individual pieces for that eventual home of your own. So there's no dodging the issue.

if it's to be modern

If you and your *true love* favor modern, you'll look for earthenware or fine china in modern shapes, in solid colors or pastel tones. Plain white, too, is wonderful to combine with colorful decorative effects on your table. For contrast with the plain colors you may want patterned salad plates, dessert plates, or cups and saucers for added interest.

for traditional living

If yours is to be a formal, traditional dining room, you'll want fine china in a simple pattern with a narrow gold band or colored border. And for a second set, for informal entertaining, do get earthenware in a scenic design or with charming floral sprays. It's a good idea to have colors that will blend with your formal china so that you can use both harmoniously for a large gathering.

or provincial, maybe

Provincial settings with warm, honey-toned furniture, pert chintz curtains, pewter or copper accessories, call for landscape scenes or for brilliant floral or fruit designs, small allover patterns, or a bright pottery in solid tones—to blend with the colors of the room.

formula for good taste

Mix imagination and good common sense in making your selection of dinnerware. Try to choose things in harmony, as you would when selecting your own wardrobe—a leather bag with a tweed suit, a silk or beaded purse with a formal gown. So with your gleaming mahogany eighteenth-century table and fine linen or organdy tablecloth you'll want delicate, formal china or fine earthenware. Or on an Early American maple table with a homespun cloth, or heavy linen place mats, you'll choose bright-colored pottery or earthenware.

The pattern should reflect you, your best judgment and that of your husband. If you don't yet know what type of furnishings you'll have, at least you do know what appeals to you, and can follow that taste in letting your china set the keynote for other things to come. It might even serve as a cue to your entire decorative scheme. If you select a simple pattern, you can always be sure that it will go well in almost any type of setting. And you won't tire of it as you might a more elaborate pattern. So when in doubt lean toward restraint rather than boldness in your selections.

rules for shopping

On your trips through the dinnerware departments you'll be continually enchanted with the galaxy of color, and fascinated by the interesting shapes you'll find everywhere. *Look* to your heart's content and revel in the freedom of selection which is yours. But when you actually get down to serious shopping, here are a few rules that you should heed before buying.

1. Consider your china only as an integral part of the complete picture which your table setting will present.

2. Actually set it up with different colored cloths, silver and glassware. Then take a good long look.

3. Ask yourself some questions: Does it delight you just to

look at it? Will it be a versatile pattern? Is it artistic? Is it a busy-busy pattern you may tire of in time? Will it mix well with other china? Analyze your answers and settle for nothing less than a "love for keeps" attitude.

4. Be sure to look at your china in the daylight as well as in artificial light. Often the entire effect is changed by a different lighting.

5. Make certain to buy from open-stock patterns so that you can add new pieces as your budget permits, and replace anything that may get broken. (Then there's no cause for tear-shedding if an accident occurs.)

6. Beware of fabulous sales. It may mean that the china patterns are being discontinued.

7. Look for the stamp of identification on the back of each piece. Certain names are outstanding for their prestige and integrity. The experts in the china departments will explain the merits of the various potters, and a sales person will gladly take you on a get-acquainted tour.

8. Buy the best quality you can possibly afford. Very cheap dinnerware is a poor investment because it chips readily and in a short time you'll have only odds and ends.

9. Buy a small quantity of good china to start with (see page 34 for minimum lists) and add to it as you can. You may want to have a breakfast set in an inexpensive ware to use until your good china is complete enough. But you'll never be sorry you invested in fine china. It is its own reward in the satisfaction it gives you always to set a pretty table.

10. Apply the same principles of design to your table settings that you would to decorating a room, with strong emphasis on co-ordination.

check these points

Don't make the mistake of judging the appearance of china by merely looking at it, nor by handling only the plates and larger pieces. Examine each separate piece to be sure it is suitable for long-term service.

Lift the cup to see whether it handles easily. Some handles are difficult to grasp and leave one feeling awkward holding them. (This is especially important to consider from the man's point of view, for he'll not be at all happy with a cup handle he can't get his finger into.)

Look at the pitchers and teapots to see that they pour well and clean easily.

Watch out for spindly legs on any piece of china, as they are apt to break off readily.

study shapes and decor

You've heard about coupe shapes, traditional shapes, lug (or covered) soup bowls and casseroles . . . but can you recognize all of them by name when you see them?

Each manufacturer has his own version of these shapes. Basically a coupe plate is rimless, with a slightly curved edge. Many are bordered in gold or platinum. Some are solid in color, plain white or with geometric or floral designs. Plates in the traditional shape usually have rims or bands. Some of these rims are fluted, some banded in gold or platinum, some in solid color or with a decoration of flowers, trailing leaves or stylized figures.

There's endless variety and we suggest that you study the

diagram which follows to familiarize yourself with some of the most popular shapes.

holloware

China serving pieces, or holloware, come in many modern shapes and are a delight to behold. Bowls are identically shaped from the little open salt to a large tureen. Covers are often interchangeable so that dishes can do double duty. (Consult diagram on pages 32 and 33.)

Among such pieces you often find solid colors and patterns with the same dominant tone so that they can be mixed and matched. For instance, there may be a teapot of plain white background with a pattern in charcoal to mix with solid charcoal cups. Or patterned serving pieces to mix with plain white dinnerware. It's a charming adventure to use your own imagination in selecting these special pieces.

oven-to-table ware

While you're about it, you must look into the handsome oven-to-table casserole dishes. You can cook, serve and even refrigerate food in them, saving time and motion. And think of the dishwashing that's eliminated. Among the most popular are the enameled cast-iron casseroles, which are ovenproof, flameproof, almost impossible to break, and styled to go as appropriately with your china as your sterling silver. Anything from a soup pot to a pipkin comes in enameled cast iron—in soft blues or greens, or more vivid melon or red tones.

Traditional Shapes in Fine China

RIM DINNER PLATE

SAUCEBOAT

COVERED VEGETABLE DISH

SOUP CUP & SAUCER

COFFEE CUP & SAUCER

DEMITASSE

SUGAR BOWL

CREAM PITCHER

COFFEE POT

TEA POT

Contemporary Shapes in China

COUPE DINNER PLATE

SAUCEBOAT

COVERED VEGETABLE DISH

COVERED SOUP

COFFEE CUP & SAUCER

DEMITASSE

SUGAR BOWL

CREAM PITCHER

COFFEE POT

TEA POT

Hint for these on your gift-preferred list, too, so your first casserole dinners will be done up in style.

You'll probably want two or three sizes—one large casserole for a main-dish meal, individual casseroles for soups, custards or meat pie, and one of the divided dishes for serving two or three kinds of foods.

how much to buy

It's seldom that anyone purchases a complete dinner service any more or even buys by the dozen or half dozen. Rather, you'll start buying place settings in fine china (consisting of one dinner plate, salad plate, bread and butter plate, teacup and saucer), or starter sets in earthenware or pottery (service for two or more), both of which can be added to as your budget permits.

More often, it's your way of life and the available shelf space which will determine how much you buy. However, you know that the very minimum for a beginning is service for you and your husband. This means two dinner plates, two cups and saucers, two salad plates, two bread and butter plates, two cereal dishes. You need also some sort of a bowl to serve vegetables, a chop plate or platter, a creamer and sugar. But what happens when you have a guest? You don't plan to be alone all the time.

service for four is the minimum

Actually, the real minimum would be service for four, with possibly extra cups and saucers and salad or dessert plates.

These can be of a different but harmonizing pattern for variety, if you wish. You can double up by using the same size plates for breakfast, for luncheon, and for salad and dessert at dinner. You can get along with this sort of an arrangement for a few months, if you don't plan to do much entertaining. But soon you'll need more and this is the amount to aim for, all you may need for some time.

service for eight as an aim

> 8 dinner plates (10 inches in diameter)
> 8 salad plates (7 inches in diameter)
> 8 bread and butter plates (6 inches in diameter)
> 8 soup plates (or cream soups and saucers)
> 8 dessert plates (like the salad plates)
> 2 vegetable dishes
> 6 cereal bowls
> 1 large platter ⎤ not necessary if you have them
> 1 small platter ⎦ in silver. Substitute one large
>   chop plate.
> 8 cups and saucers

In addition to the pieces in the list above, you'll need a cream pitcher and sugar bowl as well as a tea or coffeepot. (You may have these in silver, if you wish.) And if you like to serve after-dinner coffee, you'll want the proper small cups for it. However, they don't need to match your other china. It's more conversational when each cup is different, and you can start an interesting collection by buying that way. If you'd prefer eight matching ones, you might choose a solid color that blends with the rest of your china.

As you can see, this is a flexible list for you to add to or delete, according to your needs and how you live.

bring him in on the big decision

When (after many lunch hours of browsing) you have narrowed your choice down to two or three favorite dinnerware designs, that's the time for you to take your fiancé (or your husband) by the hand and let him help you make the final selection.

You'll find that he has some pretty decided ideas on what he likes. And he'll be apt to show good taste, too. Most men prefer an uncluttered look, clear colors, conservative shapes and styles.

When the big decision is made, if you are bride and groom-to-be, you'll hurry to register your choices with the Wedding Gift Consultant so that friends will be able to include place settings in their gift selections for you.

Then you yourselves can complete your settings with wedding-gift money, perhaps. Isn't that a happy thought?

how to care for your china

Fine china is not fragile, so don't save it for special occasions. Use it every day and enjoy it.

In preparing china for washing it is a good idea to rinse all soil off with a water spray. Or scrape the dishes with a soft brush or rubber wiper. Wash as soon after use as possible.

Washing instructions are simple. Use a mild, pure soap in warm water. Avoid harsh detergents that would be hard on the decoration of your china. Gritty cleaners or steel wool should never be used.

Drain on a rubber rack. If you haven't one, place a rubber mat or towel on the drainboard. A towel on the bottom of the dishpan also protects china.

Don't overload your shelves. Don't stack two or three sizes of plates together. The best trick is to have a rubber rack so designed that your plates can stand upright in your cupboard. Then you can remove each separately without one touching the other.

If you must stack plates, put ones of the same size together, separating each with paper or cloth circles (a paper napkin will do). Hang cups separately or stack them in twos, never more.

Use cellophane covers for the china not used every day so that it will not get dusty and will always be ready for use. You can buy these covers according to plate size or you can make them yourself.

Don't put china in the oven as the drastic change of temperature may cause it to crack. And don't ever store food in the refrigerator using your best dishes.

Rinse vinegar, lemon or salt at once from dishes which are decorated with gold, silver, platinum and colored overglaze patterns, in order to avoid discoloration.

On raised decorations of enamel, gold, silver or embossing use a soft brush.

To guard against surface scratches, do not allow aluminum or silver to rub against the china while washing it.

CHAPTER III

SELECTING YOUR SILVER

IT'S LIKE A REAL TREASURE HUNT WHEN YOU START SHOP-
ping for your silver pattern. You'll view all the shining
beauties of design, molded from this precious ore, against a
backdrop of gleaming black velvet (that's the usual method
of store display today). And from this array you'll have the
thrill of selecting one special pattern for your very own.

An important, lifelong decision it is, and certainly not one
to be taken as a mere matter of course. So the more informa-

tion you have to fortify you for this assignment, the better sat-
isfied you will be with the outcome.

Whether it is to be a sterling pattern or silver plate, select
it with love and care. As the ads all say, next to the man of
your dreams, your silver will be your most valued possession
down through the years.

first steps

Current magazines abound with ads featuring all the leading silver patterns. After studying them carefully, select your
special favorites. Evaluate them one against the other, then
check them with your fiancé or husband to see what ones he
favors. When your choices finally narrow down to one or
two, the decision should definitely be made by the two of you,
with no outside influences.

Like your other possessions, your silver should fit in with
the type of life you plan to lead. Listen to the opinions of
others if you wish, but don't be swayed away from your own
natural choices and best judgment.

Make dress-rehearsal tests of the silver you like best; try it
on different types of tablecloths, with china and glass. Look
at all the various pieces. Check to see if you like the design
as it appears on a large serving piece as well as on a cocktail
fork.

Hold each piece in your hand and make sure it feels comfortable in use. Then when you know you love it enough that
you'll delight in its beauty *every day* from that day forth, make
it yours.

rich in tradition

Silver seems to be all wound round with history. It has been called the "queen of metals" and is almost as old as civilization itself.

As a craft, silversmithing dates back to 2500 B.C., according to decorations cut in stone unearthed by Egyptian excavations. Hand-wrought silver bowls, vases and similar pieces which go back as far as 1900 B.C. are shown in museums around the world.

But the evolution of eating utensils was a rather slow process down through the ages. The knife, fork and spoon as we know them now in silver are barely a few hundred years old. It was only when primitive man discovered that his fingers were inadequate for eating a meal that he developed implements and utensils.

spoons came first

The spoon still holds first place among silver manufacturers, as it is always the initial piece to be designed in any new pattern. Spoons were formed originally by attaching wooden or bone handles to cockleshells, washed down from the sea. Later the implements were fashioned from flint, stone, wood and ivory.

In some parts of the world bronze and gold were used to make spoons. Spoons made of silver were restricted to kings and nobility, and remained so for many centuries.

Silver spoons were so rare even in later days that guests carried their own eating utensils with them wherever they went. That's when the folding spoon came into fashion. Around

1700 there was even a combination spoon, fork and toothpick which was carried.

Folding spoons remained popular until the end of the eighteenth century. It then became unnecessary to carry them because of the increased wealth created by the Industrial Revolution. This enabled more and more people to own enough additional silverware to set their *own* tables for entertaining.

forks followed

The fork did not come into general use until the early sixteenth century in Italy. Before that time it was used only for eating special dishes and delicacies. It was not taken up immediately by the common people because it was regarded as effeminate. Forks with one, two, three and four prongs were among the early models, but the two-pronged were the most common. It was not until the seventeenth century that the fork was adopted for use in England.

double-duty knives

The knife was not regarded primarily as an eating utensil until the Middle Ages. It began by doing double duty, and we find that the knife which served as a weapon, carried in a scabbard, also was used at mealtime for eating.

Table knives were first made with a broad or spatulate end to the blade, opposite the cutting edge. They were also carried by the guest who dined out and were recommended at that time "for the eating of pease and jelleys." It was only after knives became an acceptable part of the table setting that they were made in silver.

Those who could not afford silver used knives, forks and spoons of pewter.

sterling standardized

The word *sterling* as the mark of quality for silver dates back to Edward I of England, for in 1335 he decreed that all silver must be of uniform quality. It was discovered that pure metallic silver is too soft for practical use, but this difficulty was overcome by adding (or alloying) a small portion of copper to the pure silver before the craftsman began to work with it.

The accepted standardization called for 75 parts of copper to every 925 parts of silver and this weight has been recognized as the ideal quality for all purposes.

Later Edward I decreed that the craftsman's name or mark be placed alongside the mark of sterling on each piece of silver made. This identification has made English silver most valued today.

american silver

There was a remarkable group of silversmiths among the early settlers of this country, including Thomas Howard at Jamestown in 1620. Then there were John Hull of Boston and, of course, Paul Revere, who is as famous for his silver designs as he is for his historical midnight ride.

In 1868 one of the leading American silver companies (there were many then in operation in New England) adopted the English sterling standard. Other manufacturers followed suit. But it was not until 1907 that the National Stamping Law was passed so that now the quality of sterling can be definitely assured.

is sterling costly?

New methods and techniques have enabled the silversmiths to produce silver at a fraction of the cost of earlier days, so that what was once the property of only a few is now the birthright of many.

Sterling silver is still the most expensive flatware, but it is solid silver that will last as long as you live and longer. Your china and glass may eventually break, your linens wear out, but your silver will be there forever. Since it carries these long-lasting qualities, it is a sound investment that carries over many years.

Convenient budget plans for buying silver are in operation in most retail stores. Many stores will design a budget to suit each individual's need. For instance, you may buy only a place setting, consisting of knife, fork, teaspoon, salad fork, butter spreader and cream-soup spoon. Or you may purchase your entire set at the start, and pay for it on the installment plan as you use it.

Remember that sterling is the best you can buy, will last forever and it will never need replacing.

Sterling patterns are rarely discontinued, and sets may be added to as the years go by. Even many old patterns of by-gone days are available on special order through your jeweler, if he is given a tracing of the pattern or one of the pieces to match.

Everyone agrees that there is a wonderful sense of pride and satisfaction in owning sterling silver, and that makes it worth while from the start.

period designs

You don't need to be too concerned about matching your silver pattern to the exact period of your other furnishings. The principle that anything of good basic design is correct in any setting holds particularly true of tableware. You will choose a motif that blends well with your other appointments and that becomes your way of life.

Period designs are important for background study in order to be well informed on the silver subject. Silver bears the style of decoration characteristic of a particular historical era.

Most of today's period patterns belong to one of these four: Renaissance, Georgian, American Colonial and Victorian.

The Renaissance (1443-1688): elaborate designs incorporating the acanthus leaf, fruit, shells, husks, scrolls and pendants were characteristic of this period as are today's Renaissance designs in sterling.

French

English

Georgian (1714-1830): this period was named for the four
successive kings named George who ruled England at
that time. Georgian silver designs embody the popular
motifs of this period—urns, shields, rosettes, scrolls,
shells and the gadroon border.

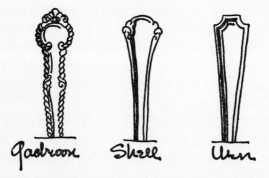

American Colonial (1620-1825): the almost Spartanlike ex-
istence of the early American settlers and their puri-
tanical temperament resulted in simplicity of design
in all things—houses, furniture and silver. It was not
until the nineteenth century that the Georgian influence reached America. Then the pure classic forms

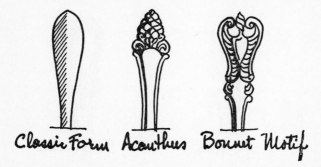

appeared with beautiful engraving. Some of the co-
lonial-inspired motifs are the urn, broken pediment or
bonnet top, and the pineapple and acanthus finial.

Victorian (1837-1901): designs of this period were inspired
by Queen Victoria's reign. Gay, graceful curves and
elaborate ornamentation revealed the grandeur that
marked these times. Flowers, fruits and flowering
scrolls characterized much of the silver.

Scroll   Shell   Flowers

Contemporary design differs from period design in that it
does not particularly seek its inspiration from any historical

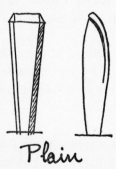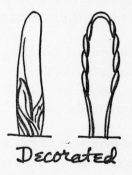

Plain   Decorated

era. Today's contemporary sterling designs are characterized by simplicity, fluidity of line and daintiness of motif. Many are severely plain. Flower and leaf motifs are among the most popular forms of decoration used.

what appeals to you?

As a rule, a simple pattern is more desirable because of its adaptability to ornateness and design of other companion pieces on the table.

If you prefer ornate silver, then select simple designs in china and glassware to carry out an artistic effect.

some objections answered

If you do favor a plain silver pattern, someone has probably sounded a discouraging note by telling you that plain silver scratches badly.

Or if you prefer ornate styles, you may hear: "Oh, it's lovely, but do you have the patience to clean it?"

The fact is that no one sterling pattern is much easier to clean than another. (See end of chapter for care of silver.)

Here's what you should know about silver patterns:

Ornate: the natural darkening, or oxidation, in the recessed areas of an ornate design is not an objectionable factor, but is intended to be that way to bring out the detail of the pattern.

Plain: the thousands of tiny scratches which a plain pattern receives during daily use give a handsome patina and mellow finish that cannot be duplicated by expert silversmiths and is something of which to be proud, not ashamed.

better be wise

Foresight is better than later regret, so check these points before you buy.

1. Weight is one of the most important things to consider when buying sterling. There are medium-weight patterns and heavyweight patterns. The heavyweight is naturally more expensive since it contains more sterling. Usually the richly ornamented patterns are in the heavyweight class.

Examine the sides of the forks and spoons to determine their thickness. By comparison with other patterns this will give you an indication of whether the weight is heavy or medium.

The majority of flatware today is in the medium- or average-weight bracket. This does not mean the weight is at all light, but rather that it's in the medium-price category. Medium-weight sterling is still heavy enough to withstand generations of wear.

2. Another determining factor on price is the amount of handwork which has been given to the silver pieces. Hand-wrought silver, which is done almost entirely by hand, is the most expensive. Hand-finished is something else. In producing sterling flatware the design is stamped on each piece by the die method. If the pattern requires hand-finishing to complete its beauty, the cost is more and depends on the intricacy of the pattern.

3. Study very carefully the designs of the patterns you are considering. Since your tableware lasts a lifetime you want to be sure that the design will never go out of style. To recognize good design, first, look for good proportions and good contour. Even an untrained eye can sense the look of harmony and symmetry in pieces of silver. Second, look for good balance. You'll find that in well-designed spoons, forks and knives good balance is immediately sensed by the even distribution of weight when the pieces are held in the hand. Notice the evenly balanced tines of the forks, and the feel of well-designed knives.

4. One of the most essential points to remember is to buy your silver from a reliable dealer who will advise you unbiasedly. There you will find the best selections of patterns in good taste—those that will never go out of date and are made by well-established silversmiths. Learn to recognize the trademarks of the reliable silversmiths. Solid silver, stamped with the sterling mark and the maker's name, gives you assurance of quality and excellence of design.

5. To keep yourself from getting into a confused state by looking at a hundred and one different patterns on display at the dealers, do have in mind several of your choice ones before you go shopping. It is always possible to browse for ideas before asking a salesman to show you "specifics." You'll find that most of the silver flatware displays have cards indicating the names of the patterns and the price per place setting of each. That should help you along your merry way toward the selection of one pattern that most appeals to you, one that fulfills your sense of beauty and most satisfies your sense of pride.

how much to buy

How much silver you buy should be determined by what you think you will use. There is no arbitrary amount.

You must have at least two place settings for you and your husband. A place setting consists of:

1 luncheon knife	1 salad fork
1 luncheon fork	1 butter spreader
1 teaspoon	1 cream-soup spoon

If you prefer, you may have two teaspoons in your place setting instead of the cream-soup spoon and the *one* teaspoon.

In addition to the two place settings, other essential pieces are:

2 tablespoons
1 meat fork
1 sugar spoon

the minimum in flatware

As in the case of your china, your *actual* minimum should be service for four. You will need:

4 luncheon knives	2 tablespoons
4 luncheon forks	1 cold-meat fork
8 teaspoons	1 sugar spoon
4 salad forks	1 gravy ladle
4 butter spreaders	1 butter knife
4 cream-soup spoons	1 two-piece steak set

You'll have the choice of buying either luncheon knives and forks or dinner sizes in your place settings. The dinner knives and forks are larger and more expensive. Many omit these on their lists, considering the luncheon size adequate for all the entertaining they will wish to do. For formal dinners, the dinner size *only* should be used for the main course.

something to build toward

If you have your china in eights, you will also want to build toward that amount in silver. It could be as follows:

8 knives	4 tablespoons
8 forks	1 cold-meat fork
16 teaspoons	1 sugar spoon
8 salad forks	1 gravy ladle
8 butter spreaders	1 butter knife
8 cream-soup spoons	1 two-piece steak set
8 dessert spoons	1 two-piece salad set

The ideal set, of course, includes both dinner knives and forks as well as the luncheon size. This means that you always have available sixteen knives and forks, in case you are serving a large buffet.

special serving pieces

In addition, you'll want to acquire more serving pieces, depending on your style of living. If you serve seafood, you'll want oyster or cocktail forks. If you serve demitasse, you'll want the small coffee spoons. You might like to have these in a different pattern, or have a collection of various ones. Then there are cake knives, cheese servers, pickle forks, etc., all of which are nice to have.

The following chart will be helpful in showing you each piece of flatware and its use. Some are really quite versatile. Study the diagram and decide what is best for you to add as you can to your basic set.

how silver plate originated

The plating of silver in Sheffield, England, came about quite by accident when an English mechanic mending a knife in 1743 happened to fuse copper and silver so that one side of the knife had a copper surface and the other silver.

This revolutionized the silver industry. And at an appropriate time too, for sterling silver was so expensive that only the nobility and families of great wealth could afford it. Sheffield plate was the original substitute for solid silver and it also replaced pewter. The process was terminated in 1836, however, with the discovery of electroplating.

By the electroplating process, which is now in universal use (and known as silver plate), a layer of silver is electrically deposited on a base metal. The finest silver plate you can buy is made from refined nickel silver and is given a heavy deposit of pure silver. This method has brought down the cost so that every home, no matter what the circumstances, can afford to have silver on the table.

how the best is made

The value of silver plate lies in the thickness of the silver coating and the way it is distributed. The best silver plate has balanced plate—that is, reinforcement at the points of greatest wear. For instance, forty per cent of the first plating is put on the front of a spoon, sixty per cent on the back where most of the wear comes. In addition, the back of the bowl and fork tines are given an extra plating, correctly balanced to make this point last as long as the rest of the piece.

Naturally sterling is the queen of silver. But if you feel you cannot afford it, you can get along happily with a good quality of plated ware and always set a pretty table. There are many designs from which to choose, and you should take as much pride and joy in its selection as you would if it were sterling. It has utilitarian value through the years, and should be taken care of just as sterling is. Buy the kind that bears the trademark of a reliable company, which usually carries with it a guarantee of service.

You can buy silver plate by the place setting, as in sterling silver, though it is usually sold in services for six, eight, or twelve. The fifty-two-piece service for eight is the most popular. These complete services are customarily available in tarnishproof chests. Most of the patterns are open stock so that you can always add to them, as you wish.

The old-fashioned idea of having a set of silver to use for every day, saving your sterling for company, is a fallacy. Sterling is practically indestructable, and as with pearls, its beauty actually increases with use. If you can afford sterling, you shouldn't hesitate to buy it and use it every day.

Silver Flatware and Its Uses

place setting pieces

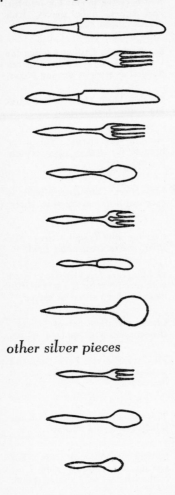

Dinner knife and fork: Necessary for the formal dinner and when more than one knife and fork are required for a meal. Fork can also be used as a serving fork with the tablespoon.

Luncheon knife: Used for all informal meals and luncheon, for meats, fish course in formal meals.

Luncheon fork: For luncheon and all informal meals, fish course in formal meals, vegetables, meats, salads, for pastries, desserts.

Teaspoon: For coffee, tea, cereal, creamed vegetables, desserts, fruit cocktail and also for bouillon.

Individual salad fork: For salad, fish, pastries, cold meats.

Butter spreader: For spreading butter, jam or jelly; for cheeses, relishes, hors d'oeuvres.

Cream soup spoon: For soups or bouillon in cups or small bowls; for serving sauces or mayonnaise.

other silver pieces

Cocktail fork: For all types of seafood cocktail, or as a lobster fork; can also be used for fruit cocktail.

Dessert spoon: Can be accompanied by dessert or salad fork for dessert; or used alone for desserts, cereals, soup, and as a small serving spoon.

Demitasse spoon: For serving coffee in small cups; as a blender for Old Fashioneds; a baby's feeding spoon.

other silver pieces—continued

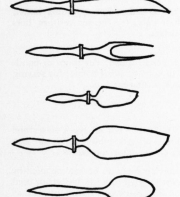

Iced beverage spoon: For iced tea, iced coffee, milk shakes, fruit drinks; stirrer for drinks.

Salad servers: Fork and spoon for serving salads from a bowl or can be used as separate serving pieces.

Carving knife (large): For carving roasts, fowl, ham.

Holding fork (large): This is for holding the roast or fowl securely for the carver.

Meat slicer: Long narrow blade is excellent for making thin slices.

Carving knife (regular size): For small roasts, steaks and fowl.

Holding fork (regular size): Used with carving knife as a server after meat has been sliced or carved.

Cheese knife: Serves cheese, cheese spreads or molded jellies.

Pie or cake server: For cutting and serving pies, cakes, aspics, frozen desserts.

Tablespoon: A serving spoon for salads, fruits, and desserts.

Serving or cold-meat fork: For serving cold meats, chops, or forms salad set with a salad spoon.

other silver pieces—continued

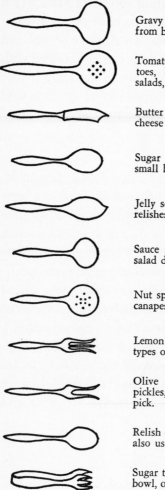

Gravy ladle: Serves gravies, or sauces of any kind from bowls or boat-shaped dishes.

Tomato server: Used not only for serving tomatoes, but poached eggs, pancakes, individual salads, food served on toast.

Butter knife: For serving butter or can be used on cheese tray.

Sugar spoon: For use in the sugar bowl, for small bowls of sauce; or for jellies and relishes.

Jelly server: For serving jams, jellies, preserves, relishes, etc.

Sauce ladle: For cream sauces, whipped cream, salad dressings.

Nut spoon: For serving nuts, candies, and small canapes.

Lemon fork: For lemon slices, pickles, various types of relishes.

Olive or pickle fork: For serving olives and pickles, also lemon slices. Can be used as a butter pick.

Relish or jam spoon: For jams, jellies, preserves; also used for serving mayonnaise.

Sugar tongs: For serving sugar lumps from sugar bowl, or small pieces of candy.

other flatware

There are metals other than sterling and silver plate which are popular too. Dirilyte, a combination of alloys, is a warm gold metal that is available in a complete flatware service and plates. Many lovely and dramatic effects can be obtained with this flatware. The design is perfectly plain, the knife blades can be sharpened, and it can be polished like silver. It is sold by the place setting and is less expensive than sterling.

stainless steel for informality

Stainless-steel flatware now comes in handsome, simple designs and has come out of the kitchen into dining-room service. It never needs polishing and is highly resistant to scratching and staining. A number of the American manufacturers of sterling silver have brought out very interesting stainless-steel designs. There are some beautiful imported ones, too.

Most of the American-made brands are moderately priced and are sold in jewelry stores and in the silverware sections of department stores. (Another evidence of its emancipation.)

It is informal, of course, and blends best with modern earthenware or pottery patterns, since most of the best designs are sleekly modern. It could well be the answer to your flatware problem while you are in the waiting period for silver and fine china.

treasured holloware

Serving pieces, such as open or covered vegetable dishes,

platters, tea and coffee services, pitchers, candy dishes, etc., are called holloware.

These are made both in sterling silver and silver-plated ware. The former, of course, is the more expensive. Many companies which make both holloware and flatware repeat the designs in the holloware. It is not necessary that the pieces match, but it is nice if they complement your table silver. Holloware is also available in Dirilyte and stainless steel.

Much to the delight of most brides, silver holloware is popular as wedding gifts. You don't need to be told that such pieces will add immeasurably to your pride of possession, as well as enhance your table settings.

For a start, you might have a double vegetable dish and a matching oval platter. The round ten-inch tray is a wonderful all-purpose little piece, which you will use from the beginning.

Candlesticks always add distinction to a dining table, and if your table is small, they are more appropriate than the more imposing candelabra. Tall candlesticks look best on a large table.

Of course, a silver tea or coffee service is a treasure to own. It lends an air of distinction and graciousness to every home. Though not a necessity by any means, it is something to work toward if you really would enjoy having one.

Sterling holloware is its own reward. But silver-plated holloware is also beautiful and very durable. Plated silver is particularly adaptable to holloware since its nickel silver base is harder and stiffer than sterling. The most desirable and more expensive silver-plated holloware is spun from highly refined nickel silver. Cheaper grades have britannia metal as a base, which is composed of tin, antimony and copper. Nickel silver-plated holloware is easily distinguished from britannia or soft metal by the clear, bell-like ring which comes when it is tapped with a pencil.

Luxurious as silver holloware may seem, it really is practical to own because many of the pieces have double uses. Here we show you how versatile some of the more popular ones can be.

Double-Duty Uses for Many Pieces

 *Salt and peppers* may double for small informal flower holders if tops are removable.

 *Paul Revere bowl* holds popcorn, nuts, or ice cubes for parties; flowers or fruit for a centerpiece. A large one could be used for punch.

 *Sugar bowl* may be used to hold cigarettes, a small flower arrangement, or after-dinner mints.

Sectioned well-and-tree platter may be used for meat and vegetables or for cake and fruit dessert for a buffet.

Silver meat platter for fowl, roasts, cold cuts—or hors d'oeuvres, salads, small sandwiches, cake.

Water pitcher with a stirrer added is impressive for serving cocktails, makes a fine vase for long-stemmed flowers.

Ice bucket holds ice cubes, may be used to chill bottles of wine, or makes a vacuum-lined casserole for hot sauces or foods.

Sauceboat may be filled with candy, nuts, olives, hot cocktail tidbits on sauceless days.

Waste bowl (from silver tea service) may be used for flowers or sauces.

Two silver shells intended for nuts and candy may be set back to back and used as a decorative flower holder.

Small silver bowls may serve as ash trays.

should silver be marked?

This is a matter of personal choice. You may have one initial or three. In the case of one, you may use either your maiden name or that of your husband. With a three-letter monogram, you'll want to include your husband's initial. If you are Mary Lou Meyers and you marry John Ashley, the initials on your silver would be MMA.

In selecting the style of lettering, be guided by your pattern. Simple letters look best on simple patterns, delicate letters on flowery designs.

The usual custom is to have the initials on the front of each piece. But if the design is very ornate and you still wish a monogram, you may have it on the back. This is a French custom which stems from the French style of table setting where spoon and forks are turned downward on the table.

Letters may be embossed (raised) or engraved (sunken). Consult your silverware dealer on the type of marking to be used. He is the best guide on choice of letters and spacing

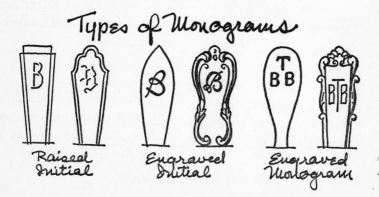

Types of Monograms

Raised Initial   Engraved Initial   Engraved Monogram and will be able to show you many tasteful ways of marking your silver as your own.

Certain holloware pieces, such as trays and bowls, tea or coffee services, are often engraved in a style all their own.

care of your silver

The first rule in caring for your silver is to use it every day. This is especially true of sterling because it becomes more beautiful with use.

Your first thought may be, "It's so hard to clean." If you live with it every day, it won't be. The hard work comes when you don't use it constantly and have to shine it up for special occasions. Rotate the use of your silver. In this way each piece gets used and washed every few days.

Wash silver soon after meals in hot soapy water. Don't overload the dishpan, or washing receptacle. You may make deep scratches by crowding it closely, one piece on top of another. Rinse in hot water. Dry with a soft cloth and be sure the silver is completely dry before putting it away.

Naturally, it must be polished occasionally, but with daily use and good care, once a month should be sufficient. Choose a good polish, rub each piece lengthwise (never crosswise or with a circular motion). Then wash in hot soapy water and rinse with clean hot water. Bring up the surface of the metal with a soft flannel cloth.

On richly ornamented silver, see that the silver polish is cleaned out of the crevices with a small brush. After each piece has been washed and dried, polish with a soft flannel cloth.

Among the foodstuffs that cause tarnish are eggs, grease, fruit juices and salad dressings, mustard, vinegar and catchup. They are the worst offenders if left on too long.

You may have heard about cleaning silver by placing it in an aluminum pan filled with a salt and soda bath or other specially prepared solutions. While both will remove tarnish from your silverware, this method is not recommended.

Some oxidation or tarnish is desired in low areas of decorative patterns to highlight the beauty of the design. A salt and soda bath bleaches out this oxidation, destroying the pleasing light-and-shadow effects of a good design.

Store those pieces which you don't use regularly in tarnishproof chests and containers. There is a tarnishproof cloth which comes by the yard, with which you can line your buffet or chests. It also comes in pocket-style rolls for flatware, in zipper-closing bags for your larger pieces and for holloware. These are good investments, and your jeweler will know about them.

Give the stainless steel blades on your knives the same care as your sterling. Do not wash the knives and forks together. The steel blades may nick the fork tines since the steel is much tougher than silver.

Scratching silverware is unavoidable. The fine tracery of thousands of minute scratchings gives your silver a soft and satiny finish, and is known as Butler finish or patina (as mentioned at the beginning of this chapter). This mellow finish, so often seen on antique silver, indicates family use and ownership, and adds charm and warmth of beauty to your silver service. So do not try to polish out these multitudinous scratches from your silver.

CHAPTER IV

YOUR GLASSWARE

JUST AS A BRILLIANT NECKLACE OR A JEWELED PIN EN-
hances a costume, so your glassware adds sparkle and beauty
to your table setting.

There is perhaps nothing quite so lovely as fragile-looking,
light-catching clear crystal stemware. And yet colored glassware with its jewellike colors, ranging from ruby red and em-
erald green to soft amber and subtle smoky shades, is bound
to be exciting to you too.

While color offers versatility and an opportunity for dis-
playing your dishes in a new light, clear glass is more dressy
and formal in appearance. So to create an interesting variation in table-setting moods, you'll doubtless want some of
both.

Glass, like china, comes from the earth, giving them a close
relationship in origin as well as in use. Both are formed into
beautiful objects under the influence of tremendous heat. Of
the two, however, glass seems the more miraculous. There
is no suggestion in a handful of sand of the transparent quality
of a beautiful goblet. But somewhere along the line there has
been a bit of magic at work.

what is the magic of its making?

No one knows exactly when the first glass was made, since it goes far back into antiquity. Tombs of Egyptian kings show pictures of glass blowers at work. In the same tombs small glass beads, which are the oldest known glass objects, were found. Early examples of glass are found among the Chinese, the Indians and the Persians. The Chinese were so impressed with the beauty of glass that they called it "thousand-year-old ice."

But it was in Rome that the greatest development of glass in ancient times took place. Egyptian glassworkers were imported into Italy, and about 14 A.D. the first glass furnace was set up in Rome. Glass then became popular among the

wealthy class. Glass cups replaced gold ones on the emperor's table. Square blocks of glass were used to pave floors.

Methods for the making of glassware were not much different from those of today. It was hand-blown into a mold; it was cut on abrasive wheels and decorated with gold; and a variety of colors were made.

venetian glass

In the early part of the fifth century Roman soldiers introduced glass to the Venetians, who became the great glassmakers of the Middle Ages. They were the first to create a style in glass and to make important contributions to color formulas.

Made mostly in Murano, an island near Venice, Venetian glass was distinguished for its lightness and graceful ornamentation. A soda-lime glass, which could be blown into all sorts of delicate shapes, was discovered there.

You are probably familiar with the exquisite Venetian-glass figurines in soft colors shot with gold, and the really handsome ash trays, vases and bowls.

By the sixteenth century Venetian glass was the fashion in Europe, and the Venetians were masters in the art of making it. The authorities were so eager to keep this monopoly that the workers were held in virtual captivity in Murano. For many years only a few apprentices were accepted. No stranger could learn the art. And any workman who carried his skill to another country was followed and ordered back.

However, some workmen did escape, and factories were established in France, Germany, Bohemia and the Low Countries, each one contributing characteristics of its own. By this development great strides were made in the techniques of cutting and engraving.

england's contribution

It wasn't until late in the sixteenth century that glassmaking came to England. In 1664 the London Glass Sellers formed a guild and supervised the work of the manufacturers, which steadily improved the quality of English glass.

Through this guild it was discovered that by using a sufficient amount of oxide of lead a clear and more durable glass would result. By enhancing the ware with facet cutting, English glassmakers originated a most distinctive product, which was at its height in the second half of the eighteenth century.

american glass

Very early in the history of our country workmen were brought over from Italy to make glass beads, which were used as money in trading with the Indians. In 1608 the first settlers at Jamestown established a small furnace near the colony's stockade, and "glass houses" for manufacturing began to appear.

In 1739 Casper Wistar started a factory in New Jersey. From here glassworkers spread to New York and New England. In Lancaster County, Pennsylvania, the name of Baron Stiegal became prominent in the history of American glass. He tried to win the American market away from foreign importations and brought over workmen from England, Italy and Germany to reproduce their native glass. His enterprise collapsed, but his workmen continued to make Stiegal forms at factories in Massachusetts, Pennsylvania and Ohio.

Stiegal glass exemplifies the charm of the colonial period and is much sought after by collectors today. It is distinguished for its excellent quality, both in clear and colored lead glass, and for the shapes of the unusual mold patterns which were in early use.

pressed glass, an american invention

The cut glass made in America in the colonial days did not compare with that made in England. But an ingenious substitute was devised, known as "three-section mold" glass. By using hinged molds in sections the popular cut-glass designs were imitated and produced at much less expense.

Called "pressed glass," this was the discovery of Deming Jarves at Sandwich, Massachusetts, in 1825, and was the means of putting Sandwich far ahead in the manufacture of glassware. Its methods of crafting have spread throughout the world as a contribution from the New World to the Old, and mark one of the very few technical changes inaugurated in glass production since the blowing of glass was first undertaken.

Through the following years the story of glass more or less parallels that of silver and china. The glass of England and Ireland (the famous Waterford glass) was of excellent quality, but designs were heavy and cutting overemphasized. Industrial development brought further advance in technical knowledge and also brought the invention of machinery which sped up the various processes.

american glass today

American glassware today is unexcelled in quality. All the rich hand-crafting art of the past is utilized and remains basically unchanged. The hand-blown glass is still executed as of old.

Now, also, there are machines that can turn out a stemmed goblet in one complete operation, and others that keep finished tumblers rolling out at top speed. These are the mass-production glasses which you'll find at amazingly low prices.

You can buy glassware at almost any price you wish to pay—from the lowest up to almost sky heights for the finest of hand-blown pieces. The simplest styles are often the most expensive. So it is well to remember that ornateness and elaborateness of design are never the criterions to use in judging quality values.

kinds of glass

Technically speaking, glass is composed of very carefully selected silica sand mixed with soda ash, potash lead or lime, and other components fused together at a very high temperature.

The two general methods of shaping molten glass are by (a) blowing and (b) pressing.

how it's blown

Blown glassware includes the lighter, more delicate stemware—that is, goblets, cocktail glasses, wine glasses, etc. Each is created in much the same manner that a blown soap bubble starts. A pipe is dipped into molten glass and a master craftsman blows the liquid into the desired shape. If a mold is used, he lowers the bubble into its cork-lined cavity and shapes the goblet bowl by gently forming and blowing.

Much of the artistry of these hand-blown pieces depends on the skill and ability of the blower, for they are the result of his own expression of line and flow, curve and contour. Since the most distinctive glassware depends solely on its shape for beauty, it is a wondrous feat to see these master craftsmen literally breathing out original designs, like artists painting pictures in the air.

Lead is one of the ingredients of blown wares, and the finer the crystal the more lead content it has. The clarity, brilliance and bell-like tone of glass is thus enhanced.

types of blown glass

There are three types of blown glass which are recognizable by their differences in quality, craftsmanship and price. All are considered in the classification of fine crystal.

1. *Offhand-blown glass* is completely hand-wrought and represents the finest and most expensive type of glass made. It is produced by expert mouth blowing without the aid of molds. All finishing and polishing are done by highly trained workmen, who have a high sense of appreciation for the sparkle and smoothness of the finished product. Almost all deli-

cately wrought pieces and very fine *objets d'art,* which you will find in the glass departments of the stores, are offhand-blown.

2. *Hand-blown glass* combines the mouth-blowing process with molding and hand fabricating. It also requires expert craftsmanship, but because of the machine work involved it is somewhat less expensive.

3. *Machine-blown glass* is fed into molds by means of an automatic feeding device and shaped by compressed air.

how glass is pressed

Pressed glass begins with a mold. Solid metal is hand-sculptured to conform to the pattern and shape desired. A "gatherer" skillfully picks up the exact amount of molten glass needed for the mold. As he forces the plunger down, the liquid glass flows evenly over the contours inside the mold. And a shapeless mass becomes a thing of beauty.

Many steps follow before the piece is complete. It receives another firing; a "finisher" with a paddle spins the piece to the finished shape; the glass is tempered and goes through many other polishing and inspection processes before it is finished.

Lime is a basic ingredient for pressed ware because it cools more rapidly and adds toughness and strength. This process is used in making stemware of all sorts and also weightier pieces such as plates, bowls, vases and sculptured forms. Pressed glass will not ring clearly when tapped, but this fact does not lessen its quality.

There are two kinds of pressed glass:

Hand-pressed glass, which is completely fabricated by hand operations.

Machine-pressed glass, which is produced by automatic methods and equipment. This type, of course, is less expensive than the hand-pressed.

decoration of glassware

You will want to familiarize yourself with the various types of decoration in glassware so that you can better appreciate what you see. There are several categories:

> etched glass
> cut glass
> engraved glass
> sand carving
> surface decorations
> of gold, silver,
> platinum or enamel

Etched glass is produced by a series of operations with strong acids which eat the designs into the glass. Plate etching is the most desirable technique used in this process. Here the design is first made on a metal plate, hand printed on specially prepared paper and rubbed down on the glass. An acid bath permanently etches the design on the glass. Some etched designs are imitated by sand blasting or enamel paint decoration. Etching is often used to produce a delicate, intricate lacelike pattern on glass.

In *cut glass* the designs are cut on a revolving stone wheel.

When the original cut is made the grinding action of the wheel leaves a soft gray, or frosted, surface on the cut portion of the glass. This is called a gray cutting. The design can be left as it is, or it can be polished until diamond-bright and transparent. When this process is used it is called a polished cutting.

Gold or platinum may be applied to glassware by brushing, stamping or by applying it and firing it into the glass. Occasionally it is burnished to produce a rich luster. Platinum requires a much hotter fire than gold.

Enameled decorations may be painted on or applied by a screen process. The enamel is then baked. It is burned into the glass so that it is permanent. Decorations on cheaper glassware are merely painted on and allowed to dry with no baking. Needless to say, this type of decoration will eventually wear off.

Engraving on glassware is done by cutting out a pattern by hand, by means of revolving wheels of copper, stone or other abrasives. The decoration usually comes out a grayish tone.

Sand carving is a modern process of creating a design through a mask on the surface of the glass by use of sand blast, or other abrasives, to produce a gray satin-finish decoration. You will see this type of décor on many bowls, plates, vases and individual *objets d'art.*

rock crystal

You may hear glassware referred to as *rock crystal,* but glassware is *not* made of crystal, and actually the term is misused. Rock crystal is really natural quartz and is not used for tableware, although there are a few very valuable rock-crystal cups and chalices which are on view at some of the museums. The term was purported to mean fine, handmade glassware that has been cut and expertly polished. Most glass manufacturers discourage the use of the term nowadays, however.

crystal

Crystal, as a descriptive word, used to mean *clear* glass as distinguished from colored glass. The name has now come to mean *all* fine, handmade glass in contrast with the cheaper, machine-made glass, regardless of color.

what goes with what?

Your dinnerware pattern should set the keynote for your glassware. In selecting your crystal pattern try to keep it in harmony with your china in scale, period and mood. Long-stemmed goblets are the most formal; cuttings add extra sparkle and brilliance; platinum or gold bands have an elegant air. Clear crystal goes with everything, but a delicate color that echoes a tone in your china can be most enhancing too.

Besides long-stemmed goblets, there are medium-stemmed and short-stemmed ones. The short are the most casual. However, the actual form of the glass isn't so important as its quality. There are some low-stemmed goblets with superb cuttings —or perhaps a bubble or a twist in the delicate stem—which are appropriate to the most formal of tables. You may use either stemmed glasses or low-footed tumblers as you please, for if the quality is there, they will be certain to dress up your table. Perhaps the most adaptable for any setting is a simple, well-shaped goblet with a moderate stem. When in doubt, this is a happy medium to strike.

For *fine china* your first choice will probably be blown lead-crystal stemware, because it is the finest available. If your china pattern has a colored rim and platinum band, you may want to consider stemware also with a platinum band. With an allover flower pattern in dinnerware perfectly plain goblets with interesting stems, or with cuttings at the base of the bowl, would be a handsome choice.

If you favor colored glass, try soft amber-toned crystal goblets, thin and artfully tapered, for a perfect combination with your gold-banded china. The soft colors in glass mingle well with delicate tones in china—pale-pink glasses with flower-sprigged china, sparkling blue goblets with blue accented or banded plates. Soft greens fit in well with leaf-patterned designs of china. Even on a formal table colored glassware is in good taste.

Fine *earthenware* calls for fine quality crystal, something with a heavy cutting perhaps (especially if it's English earthenware), or with etched decorations in a pattern or monogrammed design. Or if you wish, colored glassware which picks up the same color, or a blending tone, in your china would go well. Heed the warning (as mentioned in connection with your china and silver selections) to avoid the too-busy look of a table whose settings include an excess of patterned pieces.

For a *modern* look the tapered low goblet blends smartly with the modern coupe-shape plates. There are tapered styles that have glitteringly cut borders, engraved designs around the rims and artistic twists or bubbles in the stems. You'll find also many restrained beauties of perfectly plain design. (See sketches of Types of Goblets, pages 80 and 81.)

There are a number of crystal place settings on the market which have been made to match certain patterns in fine china and silver. Many are exquisite in design and give a pleasing and well-co-ordinated effect on the table. In making your selections, however, it is well to be alert to the fact that too many matching pieces may create a monotonous effect. This could happen, for instance, if you chose a wheat design for everything on your table—silver, china and glassware. Or if you went all out for roses in three patterns, or for fruit, or leaves.

For *less formal ware* you can create dramatic effects with color combinations. If your dishes are of earthenware or pottery—and naturally a bit heavier in appearance than fine china —you'll find pressed glass in low-footed tumblers, or perhaps hand-blown Mexican glass in complementary colors, just the answer. To go with very colorfully designed china, plain, clear crystal is perhaps the best choice, with delicate color worked in the goblet's stem or base.

A contrasting color is always effective with solid-toned earthenware or pottery. If your pottery is gray, for example, bright-blue, green or amber-toned glasses would perk up the solemnity of the gray.

Be sure to have a look at the huge double-highball glasses in a plain or crackled ware that come in deep colors—forest green, turquoise blue, amethyst—and give a very gay note when used as water tumblers on an informal table. With avocado-green pottery you might try dark-green or smoky-toned glasses. There are countless combinations that are happy choices.

Pure-white china with garnet-red glass makes a striking contrast, as does white or cream with deep blue or rich green. You may want to rely solely on your linens to create color on your table, then add the sparkle of clear crystal glassware for accent.

For *Early American or Provincial* backgrounds do consider reproductions of Sandwich glass and other pressed designs. They blend harmoniously with the period and wear handsomely too. Milk glass is available also in all sorts of interesting shapes in goblets and other accessory pieces (plates, bowls, etc.), giving a real "at home" touch to picturesque living.

guidelines for shopping

What to look for and what to avoid when you are selecting glassware.

1. Look for clarity and luster. Quality glassware is sparkling clear, whereas inferior grades have a cloudy, bluish or greenish tinge. Good glassware also has a lustrous polish which comes from repeated firings. In colored glass look for true tones and consistency in shadings.

2. Feel the edges of glasses for smoothness and regularity. Inferior glass often has scratchy edges, resulting from insufficient smoothing or polishing; also the circumference may be wavy.

3. Listen to the ring. Hold the stemware by the foot, and tap it with your fingernail. Good blown glass, containing lead,

will have a clear, rich, musical tone. Pressed glass lacks resonance, though this in no way lessens its desirability.

4. Examine the shape and symmetry. Look for well-balanced, graceful shapes with bowls, stems and feet that belong together. Clumsy shapes usually exemplify carelessness in designing and making.

5. Study the pattern. If it is etched, even the most delicate detail should be well outlined and distinct. There should be no acid spots or breaks in the lines. Look for clear brilliance as a sign of superior etching. If it is a cut piece, the cuttings should be sharp, sparkling and true. Ornamentation should follow the shape of the goblet (or whatever), and not appear to be merely "slapped on."

6. Examine for defects. No glassware is entirely free from waves, specks or bubbles. In quality glass such defects are few. Also look for, and avoid, unusually prominent mold marks or ridges on pressed glass.

7. When you are shopping for colored glassware be sure to check every piece in artificial light as well as daylight. Pale blue and lavender, particularly, lose some of their quality in artificial light.

8. The best assurance of all is the trademark of the manufacturer. Buy from a reliable one, and choose an open-stock pattern so you may be assured that it will continue to be sold over a period of time.

what determines price?

As with china and silver, the handwork required on glassware determines the price. Hand-blown stemware is the most expensive, and its price is fixed by the amount of cutting, engraving or other handwork involved. You'll recognize that such features as stems designed with blown bubbles or formed with a delicate air twist are all expensive to produce.

While the goblet that is turned out entirely by machine may lack some of the intangible charm of the hand-blown one, it still can be of good quality and good design. You'll find a great number of patterns to choose from in the medium-price bracket, many of them most artistically designed. While all glassware is breakable, it has been found that the better quality does not chip and break so readily as some of the inferior grades which are sold in the five-and-ten-cent stores.

As mentioned earlier, makers of fine glass today emphasize form and proportion in designs that play up the sheer loveliness of glass. The more distinguished glassware has no design other than its own shapeliness. Sometimes ornate decoration is at the expense of quality, so check carefully before you buy.

shapes and sizes

There are various shapes to consider when buying stemware. You'll see low goblets that taper right from the foot, others with long slender stems that naturally break more easily than the shorter, more sturdy designs. Other pieces of stemware, such as the wine glass and sherbet, are usually made in the same proportion as the water goblet. (Study shapes as shown on next page.)

Types of Goblets

LONG STEM GOBLETS

PLAIN CRYSTAL   CUT CRYSTAL   POLISHED CUT

ENGRAVED   PLATINUM BAND   DECORATED STEM   ETCHED

MEDIUM STEM GOBLETS

BUBBLE STEM   SANDWICH TYPE   MILK GLASS   WREATH CUT

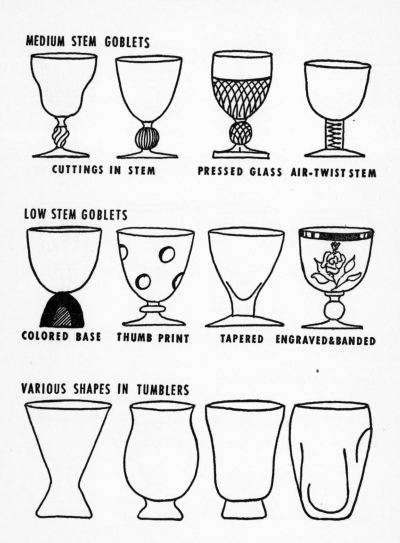

MEDIUM STEM GOBLETS

CUTTINGS IN STEM   PRESSED GLASS AIR-TWIST STEM

LOW STEM GOBLETS

COLORED BASE   THUMB PRINT   TAPERED   ENGRAVED&BANDED

VARIOUS SHAPES IN TUMBLERS

how much to buy

As with china and silver, glass is also sold by the place setting. The most popular setting consists of a water goblet, sherbet or champagne, and a medium wine glass. The sherbet may be used for champagne, sherbet, fruit or fish cocktail. The medium wine glass may double for fruit juices and cocktails.

Another choice, comprising a place setting, might be goblet, sherbet, iced-tea glass, juice glass and salad plate. Or you can make up your own selection, according to your needs.

Storage space, perhaps more than anything else, determines the amount of glassware you will buy. As with china and silver, service for four would be a minimum. It might be composed of the following:

4 water goblets	4 tumblers
4 sherbets	4 juice glasses
4 medium wine glasses	4 salad plates

If you do very much entertaining, you'll soon want service for eight in the above items. Keep in mind the versatility of each. The salad plates are suitable for serving dessert too, and need not match the other glasses if you want a change of pattern. They would be attractive in color if your stemware is of clear crystal or if they can be matched to your colored glasses. The tumblers, of course, may be used for highballs, iced tea or any cold beverage, and the juice glasses may also be used for cocktails.

You'll probably plan to have your goblets, wines and champagnes in the same pattern. The wine glass *could be* in a dif-

ferent pattern if it happens that way, but all three should be
in harmony, at least. If you serve liqueur, you'll want the correct glasses for it. Often they are chosen in a different pattern
since liqueur is served after everything is cleared away, and
very often in the living room. Sometimes the glasses match
the decanter, and can be bought in sets.

These are suggestions especially pertaining to your better
glassware. Since even the best of glass is breakable, you may
wish to provide some everyday sets for changing off. Don't
be afraid to *dress up* your table, though, even when the two of
you are alone. Choice things are made to enjoy and not to
spend their lives hidden in a cupboard.

wine glasses

A specific glass for every type of wine isn't at all necessary.
If you serve either red or white wine, you will need only one
kind of wine glass—either medium or the largest size—to suf-
fice for all occasions. This does not mean that you should
serve extra-large portions because of the size, for a wine glass
should never be more than half filled.

You can serve a perfect dinner if you have: a water goblet,
wine glass, sherry glass, liqueur. You can really splurge if you
have a secondary or smaller wine glass and a saucer champagne.

Before making your selection in wine glasses, it may be helpful to you to know that true wine lovers usually select clear
crystal in order that the color of the wine will not be distorted.
Deep colors such as dark blue, green, smoke, amber and amethyst give red wines a muddy color. Red glass is a bit more

complimentary. Light wine served in dark glasses loses its color completely. Pale-green glass is traditional in Germany for white wines, and pastel tints are acceptable everywhere for either red or white wines.

finger bowls

If you wish to add finger bowls to your list, by all means do. It's a nice custom to use them, but since they do present a bit of a problem without a maid, you may want to use them only on some special occasion when there is a very sticky dessert, fruit, or other delicacy which would require them.

Finger bowls are available in a number of open-stock crystal patterns, and also are becoming more and more popular in a wide assortment of colored glass. The bowls are convenient and attractive to use as nappies when not in use as finger bowls.

bar accessories

Making up your list of bar requirements rightfully comes under your husband's jurisdiction. He'll probably be the "mixmaster" in the family, so why not help him choose whatever strikes his fancy by going shopping with him? There's endless variety in glassware to choose from, and many styles are quite inexpensive. Some are decorated, some plain, others engraved or cut. There are novelty glasses in abundance, and whether the highball-glass pattern matches the cocktail glass, sherry glass, etc., is a matter of personal choice and taste.

Glasses for the Bar

OLD FASHIONED   HIGHBALL   DOUBLE OLD FASHIONED   COCKTAIL

TYPES OF WINE GLASSES

SHERRY 2oz.   CLARET 4oz.   CHAMPAGNE 5oz.   BURGUNDY 5oz.

CORDIAL 1oz.   BRANDY GLASSES   PORT 3oz.   SAUTERNE 4oz

Highball glasses hold fourteen to sixteen ounces and, of course, may be used for any cold beverage such as iced tea, or they may double for tumblers on the table. Old-fashioned cocktail glasses are standard size, and make nice fruit-juice glasses when not in bar service. If your cocktail glasses are to be different from your stemware pattern, you may choose one of the many sets now available with matching cocktail shaker or pitcher for martinis. If the glasses are plain, you may want to have them smartly monogrammed.

The large or medium-sized wine glass, referred to previously, may serve also as a cocktail glass.

The number of glasses you need for the bar depends entirely on how many you will be entertaining at one time, how often you entertain (with breakage in mind) and your selections in drinks. In the beginning you'll want at least six or eight each of the highball, old-fashioned and cocktail sizes, if you follow the tastes of the usual young married couple today.

companion pieces in glass

Glass is made in all shapes, forms and for practically every purpose. You may have a complete dinner service, if you desire. It's smart to include glass salad plates for desserts and summer luncheons, or for serving after a bridge game.

Take the matter of vases. You will need assorted sizes, for no home is really complete without fresh flowers on special occasions. Invest in a nice tall vase for the first cherry blossoms or forsythia branches in the spring, for stately dahlias, huge chrysanthemums, and for those gorgeous long-stemmed roses that may appear on an anniversary or birthday. Fill it with green leaves during the winter if you wish, and place it on the floor or on a casement-window ledge.

Have an in-between-size vase for daffodils, daisies and all medium-length stems. And, of course, a bud vase for one beautiful rose—for your desk, your dressing table, or coffee table. A bubble-ball vase, or huge brandy snifter, makes an artistic accouterment for floating a few blossoms or for trailing ivy vines.

There are bowls in all sizes, pitchers, cigarette boxes and ash trays. Lovely figurines can do much to enliven a table centerpiece or set off a wall bracket. Tall apothecary jars are decorative filled with flowers or candy, or just standing in majestic beauty.

Even though you may have silver candlesticks, you probably will want to consider glass ones too. Some are quite outstanding with bubble stems, twisted bases and decorated edges. Candelabra that are works of art in crystal are also desirable for your list.

We don't need to tell you what colored-glass pieces can do to a room. A red or sea-blue bottle that catches the sunlight can serve as an exciting note of color in a hallway or dining alcove. Many of these decorative bottles are quite inexpensive, too.

Crystal bowls and figurines can double as book ends. You might have a figurine at one end and a bowl filled with ivy leaves on the other. You may add pieces of glassware to highlight your bookshelves, and to accentuate the colors you wish to bring out in your rooms.

how to care for your glassware

Follow these few simple rules to add beauty and long life to your glistening treasures:

1. Never hold a piece of fine stemware under the hot-water faucet. This quick and uneven heat may cause it to crack.

2. When pouring hot liquid into a cup, bowl or glass, place a silver spoon in the receptacle first to absorb the heat.

3. Rinse milk glasses with cold water soon after use. If they have stood for some time and are sticky, rinse them with lukewarm water and a little soda.

4. Wine glasses should be rinsed or washed immediately after using so a deposit will not form.

5. Don't stack glasses one inside the other. If you do and they stick together, never try to pry them apart. Breakage can be avoided simply by pouring cold water in the inner glass and holding the outer one in warm water. They will then separate easily.

6. Let glass dishes come to room temperature before serving either piping hot or ice-cold food.

7. If you wash your glasses in a dishwasher, use the recommended type of cleanser and allow them to dry in the rack. If you wash them by hand, use one of the detergents or liquid washing agents, rinse in warm water (never scalding) and set the glasses to dry on a rubber-coated dish drainer.

8. Use a soft brush for washing cut or pressed patterns to insure getting into the deep places. Never wash or rinse gold-decorated glass with scalding water, or use strong soap, as these will loosen pure gold.

9. In handling glassware the edges should not be permitted

to bump or strike anything or one another. This will cause nicks. A tiny nick may be smoothed by rubbing carefully with fine emery paper.

10. When storing glassware, do not stack. And glasses should never be placed with the rims down.

11. Tea leaves soaked with vinegar will remove lime deposits which sometimes are found in water bottles or pitchers. Put leaves into the piece and shake around until deposit disappears. Clean vinegar cruets with diluted ammonia.

CHAPTER V

YOUR LINENS

TROUSSEAU LINENS ARE A BRIDE'S PERSONAL RESPONSIBILITY —her dowry to bring to her new home. Although modern-day materials aren't all of linen, as they were years ago, the term still applies to table coverings, sheets and towels.

You'll find yourself choosing your linen trousseau with the same loving care you show when selecting your lingerie. Whether you buy it all yourself or receive much of it as gifts from relatives and friends, you should make sure to have just what you want in colors and styles. And when it is all neatly stacked on your shelves you'll be as proud to show it off as you are your china and silver.

Make your lists for the minimum rather than the maximum amount. Linen closets can overflow with unnecessaries. While it's true that Grandmother may have had scads and scads of linens all prettied up with tatting and embroidery (much of which she never used), remember that she lived in one big house for years and didn't face the problem of moving about. So buy for your present needs and add to your supply as the situation warrants it.

LINENS FOR YOUR TABLE

In the foregoing chapters we have been discussing your china, silver and glass—the integral parts of a table setting. Now, to complete the picture, let's take up table linens first.

What an opportunity you have here to portray your own individuality! There's much to choose from—damask and laces, which are ever popular and desirable; printed and hand-blocked cloths in bright or muted tones, and linen with embroidered or openwork designs. There are place mats of linen, organdy, eyelet embroidery, plastic or cork. And for something completely individual you may want to scout around the yard-goods departments (both dress and decorating departments) for a particular color or fabric to make up yourself.

You completely change the mood of your table with different coverings. You may be boldly gay for breakfast, dainty for luncheon, and quietly dignified for dinner. The simplest food becomes tempting when served in attractive, colorful surroundings.

analyze your linen needs

As with your other table accessories—china, silver and glass
—the type of life you plan to lead and the amount of space
you have should determine the quantity of your linens. If the
social pattern you have set for yourself calls for big, sit-down
dinner parties, you will naturally need some large dinner
cloths of artistic design. But if like most young marrieds of
today you plan to entertain mostly on the informal side with
buffet suppers and small dinner groups, then you should con-
centrate on a heavier supply of smaller and more colorful
cloths and place mats of attractive variety.

To start with, if you are setting up housekeeping on a permanent scale, it is practical to have one fairly large cloth with
twelve napkins that would accommodate a gathering of family
(or friends) at holiday or anniversary time. This cloth may
be of damask, embroidered or plain linen, in white or delicate
pastel colors. It should be large enough to cover your dining-
room table when all the leaves are in place. As a guide to go
by, bear in mind that a 72- by 90-inch cloth will accommodate
a table for eight, a 72- by 108-inch cloth a table for twelve.

table damask

There are various kinds of damask. The best, of course, is
the pure Irish-linen damask. It is the most expensive but is
unsurpassed in quality and unrivaled in durability. The making of damask is the most intricate and expensive of all methods of weaving, and since there are variations in linen it is
advisable to buy damask from a store of high rating.

The best grade of linen damask is made of fine, even yarns of long-fibered flax, well twisted and firmly woven. Lower qualities are woven from short-fibered flax, which makes coarse, uneven yarns and less durable cloth.

Besides the pure linen damask, there are cloths made of carded or combed cotton combined with rayon in colors and patterns similar to those of the finer all-linen damask. The quality depends on the fineness of yarns, closeness of weave and firmness of the twist, and some qualities run higher in cost than the linen damask. The soft sheen and luster of this type of damask, particularly in pastel shades, make a beautiful effect, catching the gleam of candlelight and silver on the table. You'll discover, too, that a good white linen damask becomes even whiter, smoother and more lustrous with use.

All-cotton damask when new has an appearance similar to linen, but it is not a good investment since it does not stand up well after washing and soon gets rough and frayed-looking.

Most linen damask is laundered before it is put on the market and labeled "all pure linen, laundered, ready for use." "Linen" and "Pure Linen" labels mean that the articles so tagged contain at least ninety-five per cent linen.

In design damask usually falls into two types: *floral* and *conventional*. Select the pattern in relation to your chosen china. You will find floral patterns in all price ranges and combinations. Classic motifs and polka dots are more formal in feeling than the floral patterns and harmonize well with eighteenth-century interiors. Plain satin bands are very popular since they lend themselves to any type of table setting. But because of the utter simplicity of design the banded damask should be of fine quality.

linen and other fabrics

Much of the linen patterned with cutwork and embroidery is made from round, smooth yarns which can be readily pulled for openwork decoration. Art linen is made in the British Isles and embroidered either in China or Puerto Rico where labor costs are low. Embroidered linens when carefully made of quality fabrics are usually very serviceable and set a beautiful table. The linen may be unbleached, partly bleached, fully bleached, or dyed.

For sheer daintiness, too, you'll love the fine linens appliquéd with organdy found both in tablecloths and place mats, in white and pastel colors. White organdy cloths may be enhanced by using colored material underneath for variation.

There are handsome cloths made of synthetic fibers which are wrinkleproof and not difficult to launder. They are available in all colors and combinations; some are woven with metallic threads for extra glamour.

On your linen hunt you'll see also many cloths of solid-colored linen and with printed designs, usually in luncheon and bridge cloths. They may be entirely plain, printed, hand-blocked or yarn-dyed. Those that are *hand-blocked* are bound to be expensive since the design is made with a hand-cut wooden block and colors are applied by hand.

Some patterns are *screen-printed* with a hand-blocked effect, so when buying it is well to know the distinction and get what you are paying for. Most of these printed linens are so marked.

Hand-screen printing is the customary process used for printing better-than-average quality fabrics. Here color is applied by hand through a design on a silk screen, somewhat like a stencil. While it is a quicker process than hand-blocking, it is not produced in great volume and thus is more expensive than machine-printed linens.

Screen printing can also be done by machine, and the cloths or place mats are cheaper than those that are hand-printed. The label should designate if the article is hand-printed.

Most printed fabrics are *roller-printed,* which means that a design is etched on a copper roller and run off in quantities. Fast-color prints are produced for small cost and available to you at low prices. They are gay and serviceable for the breakfast table, appropriate and pretty with colored pottery sets.

Yarn-dyed table linens come in stripes, plaids and plain colors. The yarns are dyed before the cloth is woven, making it colorfast both to sun and laundry. The quality of yarn and closeness of weave determine the quality of the material. The better the quality the more smooth and even the weave.

lace tablecloths

The loveliest lace cloths are made of linen fibers and when well made are strong and durable. Various techniques employed in lacemaking include bobbin, needlepoint, crochet or knotting. The finest laces are still handmade, but machines now copy many of the designs so accurately that beautiful designs are available at reasonable prices.

There are many different qualities of both machine and

handmade lace, depending on the workmanship, the quality and firmness of the yarn and the elaborateness of the design. To test the character of a lace cloth for wearing quality, examine the strength of the yarn, see that the edges are firm and well finished. The lace mesh should be small enough not to catch and tear easily, the yarns even and near the same size.

Genuine lace is still handmade and will be recognized by its irregularities.

place mats of every description

There are place-mat designs for every meal—breakfast, luncheon and dinner. There are exquisite linen and organdy mats that are appropriate for dress-up occasions. Gay plaids, woven textures and plain linen are all used for both breakfast and luncheon. Then there are the plastic mats, which are a daily blessing indeed for working wives. They come in all designs, from replicas of dainty eyelet embroidery to coarse linen, and are easy to clean. They simply need to be wiped off with a damp cloth. Several sets in different colors with contrasting or harmonizing napkins made of absorbent fabric will allow alternates for breakfast.

The usual place-mat sets in the finer fabrics come with seventeen pieces, which include eight mats, eight napkins and a runner; or you can buy eight-piece sets, which include four mats and four napkins; there are also individual mats with matching or contrasting napkins. If you do not wish to use the runner (narrow tables certainly don't need them), buy the mats individually in whatever quantity you want.

for buffet service

Since serving buffet is such a popular way of entertaining, don't overlook having something special in your selections for that very purpose. Such cloths can be used also for luncheon and Sunday brunch. Buffet tables usually call for striking contrasts. You may want a fanciful print in linen or a deep color like tangerine, a bright green or blue, or even checks or plaids. With these have napkins in a contrasting color or try half of them matching, half contrasting. For example, with a pink cloth have navy-blue napkins or half pink and half brown ones; with a melon shade, avocado or hunter-green napkins.

Bridge tablecloths, selected to harmonize with one another and with your buffet cloths as well, will come in good stead when you want to entertain buffet style with sit-down service at small tables. With a figured covering on the big table, for instance, you might have solid-colored cloths in compatible colors on the bridge tables.

Tea cloths make appropriate covers for bridge tables and are a better size than the regular card-table cloths. You may want some of both sizes for various occasions.

For serving afternoon tea you'll find attractive sheer linens and organdies in both round and square cloths of fifty-four-inch size. With them you can get plain hemstitched, fourteen-inch napkins, if there are none to match the cloth as a set. White and soft pastel tones are preferred for dressing the tea table in traditional style.

cocktail napkins

There is such a wide selection of novel cocktail napkins that it is a real delight to shop for them. You'll want to have at least a dozen for small cocktail parties and for light evening-snack gatherings. When you're entertaining a large crowd you may rely on paper napkins, if you wish, as laundry savers now that they are acceptable in our casual-type living. Buy quality paper napkins which are absorbent even in the small size, and in the dinner size select the sturdy kind that have the appearance of cloth.

finger-bowl doilies

If you plan to use finger bowls—and they are becoming more and more popular with young marrieds for utilitarian reasons rather than for putting on style—you'll need the right kind of doilies. They may match your very best tablecloth or place-mat set, or they may be of a different style, as you choose. These doilies usually are made of linen, lace-edged and very dainty.

extra napkins

After you are better acquainted with your entertaining needs you will probably want to add extra damask napkins. If you select something simple, such as a plain satin-band pattern, it will be of the type to go well with everything. Fine colored napkins may be used to contrast with a white tablecloth as a change. They also combine nicely with a lace cloth.

take table measurements

Have the measurements of your table with you when you

shop. When buying dinner cloths it is necessary that you know the table's width and length, with and without the extension leaves. All cloths, whether damask, lace, or linen, should overhang a minimum of twelve inches. Buy round cloths for round tables and allow for the same length overhang, or longer.

When buying place mats consider the size. They should be large enough to hold an entire place setting: plate, glasses, silver, salad plate, bread-and-butter plate. In placing them on the table, two feet should be allowed from the center of one place setting to the center of the next to avoid crowding. Round doilies are best on a round table; a rectangular table takes square or oblong ones best. If a table is narrow, you might consider using a runner on either side and leaving the center section bare. If your table is rather long and narrow, it makes an interesting arrangement to use several runners crosswise of the table and left hanging on either side.

table pads

With a damask cloth, either linen or rayon, a table pad is necessary. Folding asbestos pads, which are made to order for the table, are particularly good since they protect the finish of the table when hot dishes are placed on it. These are covered with felt on one side and a moistureproof fabric on the other in either a wood-grain finish or white. This type pad should be ordered to measure at the linen counter to fit the table when used with, or without, leaves. The pad can be folded and stored in a drawer when not in use.

There are those who still prefer to use a soft white silence cloth under a damask dinner cloth, and it does give body to the cloth. Silence cloths also may be ordered at the linen counter, according to your table specifications.

You'll need to place individual heatproof pads under hot dishes to protect the table when you are using place mats or sheer cloths. There are many attractive kinds—in silver, brass, straw, pottery and ceramics; also wrought-iron trivets and decorative tiles. Choose the type that goes best with your other table appointments.

select color with care

Keep your dishes in mind when selecting background colors for them. Very simple or plain-colored dishes are striking against bright, block-print cloths. Remember, however, that machine-printed cloths, while a fraction of the cost of the hand-blocked, are likely to be rather bold in color and design, and need to be selected with care.

If your dishes have a strong, multicolored pattern, pick out just one of the colors and match the cloth to it in a solid tone. You might like a rose tone to bring out the flower color in the design, for example, or a deep green to accent the china pattern. Have variety in your linens so that you may change table backgrounds often.

Your dinner table should express serenity after the busyness of the day, so why not make it pretty with light pastel tones? Or have a lovely gray-tone cloth, which offers a quiet setting for rich-colored flowers both in china and in centerpiece.

Dark colors are also pleasing. Deep-wine coverings are effective with patterned china that picks up the same red in flowers or in a more classical design on a white background.

Shades of pink are flattering to most china patterns, except those with yellow decorations which are complemented best by light green or gray.

selecting monograms for your linens

You may want to add a personal touch to your linens by having them monogrammed. Since your tablecloth for a service for six should measure two and a half yards, allowing twelve inches for overhang, the place for the lettering will depend on the pattern of the cloth. Also, you don't want the monogram to fall in a spot on the table top where it would cause the dishes to stand unevenly. It may be applied in the center of the cloth, or near a corner where it is seen only as guests enter or leave the room. You will have to decide whether you want a simple or fancy monogram. Script is always in good taste.

For a tablecloth monograms should be from three and a half to five inches long.

Dinner napkins, which are twenty-two inches square, require lettering two or three inches long. Since the napkin usually is folded in thirds, the monogram may be in the exact center, if the design frames it, or it may be toward the corner. Satin-banded napkins always lend themselves well to monogramming by having the letters placed on the band in the center of one side of the napkin.

On luncheon napkins and smaller tea napkins the monogram is usually embroidered in the corner, then the napkin is folded in such a way that the corner is on the outside. On place mats initials may be at the top and upper left.

The same rules apply to the letters used in your linen monogram as those given for your silver. It used to be the custom for a bride's linen to carry the initials of her maiden name, and some linen shops still recommend it. (Stores have had a few trying experiences when an engagement was broken after the linens were monogrammed with the initials of the husband-to-be and had to be changed at great expense.) Though the use of maiden initials is still quite correct, the modern trend is toward the monogram which includes the initials of the girl's first name and surname, coupled with the initial of the surname of her husband-to-be. When Helen Jackson marries Allen Black the monogram probably would be HBJ. Usually the last initial is given prominence by being placed in the center and made larger. (See sample monograms, page 61.)

make your table coverings

With a bit of imagination and ingenuity you can make some of your own cloths and place mats. If you can't find the color or texture you want in ready-made pieces, browse through the upholstery or yard-goods departments. There you'll find deep colors in linen, heavy materials like burlap and felt and many interesting textures that will make up well into individual mats or cloths.

If you are adept with the needle, you can achieve beautiful effects with fine linen on which are sewn contrasting bands of color, edgings of braid or fringe. There are also a number of materials that can be self-fringed satisfactorily instead of being hemmed.

If it should be your lot to receive an excess of white table-cloths, it's a simple matter to tint some of them. Pastel tones come out better than dark colors, which should be dyed professionally.

a list to start you off

Following is a list of linen needs for your table that will cover most social functions in a limited way. Some of the items may be expanded, others may be eliminated to fit your way of life.

> 1 dinner cloth, 12 napkins (cloth of correct size for table, as measured, with and without leaves; round cloth for round table)
> 2 breakfast cloths, or 2 sets of place mats, with appropriate napkins
> 2 luncheon cloths with napkins
> 2 place-mat sets for luncheon and dinner
> 2 cloths for bridge table and tea table with napkins
> 12 cocktail napkins

what are your specific needs?

For an efficiency apartment: In this case you'll probably have a small dining table in a dinette or a folding table in the living room. If you can seat six at the table, you'll need a two-and-one-half yard cloth with napkins. It may be of white damask or one of pastel shades; or, if you prefer, a plain or embroidered linen, or a lace cloth for best.

You'll want at least one cloth in a solid color and one or two prints or plain dark colors for serving buffet suppers.

If your table is small, card-table size, consider buying an extra round (or square) portable top which so conveniently makes a table larger. A round cloth with a deep overhang would be suitable for this type of table, never place mats, as the portable top needs to be covered.

You may want more place mats than tablecloths for general use, since they are easier to launder. Fabric, as well as plastic ones, will come in handy for many purposes, such as serving suppers on small tray tables in the living room (while watching television) and for breakfast trays.

Then make note, too, of a couple of bridge sets or tea cloths for special occasions.

For an apartment (or house) with a dining room: You will probably have a regulation-size dining table or drop-leaf table that opens up to regular size in this type home. A really good damask cloth, three yards in length, with twelve napkins won't go amiss here. Or, as mentioned before, the covering may be of linen with lace or embroidery, Madeira-type.

For serving six at a sit-down dinner you might add a two-and-one-half-yard cloth in cotton and rayon damask or linen, or a fine quality print. And for buffet suppers choose a colorful cloth (one or more, depending on how often you entertain buffet style). Three place-mat sets should be sufficient to start with for luncheon and dinner use, chosen especially for showing off your china and silver to advantage. You'll need a collection of plastic mats, too, for everyday breakfast and luncheon use.

how to care for your linens

If you have beautiful linens, treasure them and take good care of them when in use and when in storage.

Before washing remove any stain which might become set in the material. Candle wax can be picked off when dry; if soaked into the cloth, use benzine gasoline, carbon tetrachloride, or a similar cleaning fluid.

To remove fruit-juice stains, stretch the fabric taut and pour boiling water from a height. If this does not remove it, try covering the stain with glycerine and repeat with hot water.

Use a bluing made from aniline dyes. Some bluings contain iron and cause rust stains on linen. Acetic acid or vinegar will usually remove such a rust stain.

For mildew stains use a mild bleach, such as Javelle water, on white linens. It may remove the color of dyed fabrics, however.

If wine is spilled on the cloth, cover the spot at once with salt and wash thoroughly afterward. If the stains are old ones, wet with suds of yellow laundry soap, coat with powdered starch and bleach two hours in the sun.

Always remember that any fluid strong enough to remove stubborn stains is almost sure to remove color from tinted fabrics so should be used only on white materials.

In laundering, use a bland soap and avoid any severe rubbing. The biggest problem in caring for linens is the laundry. While most cloths—that is, those of good linen fabrics—may be washed in a machine, you must be prepared for long hours at the ironing board. Place mats are, of course, easier to iron.

Linens should be ironed first on the wrong side while quite damp; for heavy linen this is a must. Use a moderately hot iron because linen scorches easily. It has more sheen if ironed on both sides, first on the wrong side until partially dry, then on the right side until completely dry. Either white or colored damask should always be ironed on both sides.

For other fabrics containing rayon or synthetic fibers follow washing and ironing instructions that come with the cloth. Anything with rayon in it takes a warm iron, never hot.

Embroidered linens should be ironed face down on a terry towel or any soft foundation to bring out the design.

Lace cloths generally may be used a number of times before washing. Most spots can be removed without leaving a ring. After washing the cloth in a mild suds wrap in a towel to absorb excessive moisture and hang evenly on a line. Pull it gently to its original shape, watching the edges, and when dry, shape and smooth it carefully. Lace cloths may also be dried on a curtain stretcher.

In a good commercial laundry soft water, heavy suds and controlled temperatures are used. Table linen is usually ironed in a flatwork ironer to give it a good finish. If the laundry does handwork, damask cloths are ironed by hand at a higher rate than machine-ironed pieces.

Dark-colored cloths of most fabrics are more of a nuisance to launder than white or pastel since they have to be done separately. However, some of the deep-toned cloths of synthetic fibers are easy to launder and are wrinkle-resistant.

Bedroom Linens

Along with the thrill of acquiring stacks of snowy-white sheets for your trousseau, there is the added attraction of having color and novelty designs to spark up your basics in bed linens.

Sheets now boast flower sprigs, colored stripes and plaids in borders and in allover patterns. Blankets have interesting borders of striped ribbon or chintz and, like the sheets, they come in allover stripes and flowery patterns. Desirable too are blanket covers of nylon (no ironing required) in soft-hued tones, bed pillows covered in pastel tones, and myriads of styles in ready-made bedspreads with gay dust ruffles.

Definitely designed to make life easier for you, as well, is today's miraculous fitted sheet. It goes over the mattress like a slip cover, allows plenty of toe room, minimizes bedmaking. This sheet simply does not pull out or wrinkle but stays snugly in place with its mitered corners.

Whatever else you may feel you have to skimp on, don't let it be the quality or size of your bed linens. The best you can buy will prove an economy in the long run in both wear and satisfaction.

sheets and pillowcases

What fabrics are best?

Muslin and percale are the principal fabrics used in making sheets and pillowcases.

Linen is in a luxury class quite by itself, and though expensive, linen sheets will wear for many years and are a delight for their coolness in summer.

Muslin sheets are less costly than percale but are not nearly so soft and light. Their quality may be coarse or fine, depending on the size, texture and number of yarns used in the lengthwise and crosswise yarns of the fabric.

Percale sheeting is not quite so strong as heavyweight muslin but is preferred by most people because of its smooth texture and light weight. Finer yarns are used in percale and the sheeting is more closely woven than muslin. If your laundry is to be paid for by the pound, you will find that percale sheets cost less to launder.

How to Judge Quality

The *thread count* is important to consider when buying sheets. This means judging values by the number of threads in one square inch of sheeting fabric. Sheets with a count of under 180 per square inch are muslins (the heavyweight muslin has 140 count); those of 180 or more are percales. Percales in the medium price have a thread count of 180. The finest percales are 200 or more and have an almost silky feeling.

You often will find sheets labeled as to type number, indicating the thread count of the sheet. For example: Type 200 is the fine percale, having 200 or more threads per square inch. A sheet woven with approximately the same number of threads of the same quality and size in both warp and filling is referred to as a "balanced fabric" and is expected to give more balanced wear. ("Warp" is lengthwise threads, "filling" is crosswise.) To determine a sheet's potential wearing qualities, examine it carefully and read information given on labels.

Weights of sheets are usually stated on labels. They vary from about three and a fourth to five and a fourth ounces per square yard.

Sizing refers to starch, china clay, or other finishing materials which give a smooth surface to new sheets. Some sizing is necessary on the lengthwise yarns to keep them from breaking in the loom. Look for markings of "No Weighting" on sheet labels to guarantee that no overdose of starch has been used. To determine this, rub parts of the sheet together over a dark surface. If a white powdery substance comes out, it indicates that the sheet is sized. If it is heavily sized, it will be sleazy after the first washing when the sizing is removed. Sizing percentage is generally stated on labels that carry weight tabulations in order that you may know the amount of cotton contained in the fabric. If sheets are of the same quality except for weight, the heavier fabric may be expected to wear longer.

Breaking strength indicates the number of pounds of pull necessary to break one inch of the fabric. In testing for strength, if the breaking strength of one sheet is forty pounds and another one is sixty pounds, naturally the sixty pound is the stronger.

The *grade of cotton* used and the combing, spinning and weaving all are important in the appearance of a sheet. The better ones are woven of combed, long-staple cottons. To compare sheets for yarn quality, hold them up to the light and notice the difference in smoothness and firmness of the various types. Feel the fabrics for smoothness and even texture.

The *selvage* should be examined. Good sheets are made with a tape selvage, which should be firm, strong, clean and neat, with no loose threads. *Hems* also indicate the type of workmanship evident on a sheet. They should be stitched straight with small, even stitches (at least fourteen to the inch), and the ends should be closed. Top hems are usually three inches wide on muslin, four inches wide on percale sheets. Bottom hems are one inch wide. Often hems of the same size on both ends are available. Hemstitched hems, thought desirable on fine sheets, have a tendency to tear off before the sheet is worn out.

sheet and pillowcase sizes

Jot down the measurements of your bed, if possible, before you go shopping. If you are buying sheets that are not fitted, make sure that they are long enough to avoid strain on the fabric, and allow for tuck-in at the foot of the bed and a fold-over at the head.

Sheets for average-sized beds are made in a variety of lengths ranging from 90 to 113 inches. The recommended length for the average-length bed is 108 inches. The dimensions marked on a sheet refer to the *torn length* before hemming. Hems take up from four to seven inches, and allowance must be made for a shrinkage of six per cent or five inches since sheets in this country are *not* preshrunk. (In Canada sheet sizes are stated in *finished lengths,* and some are preshrunk.)

The width of a sheet is equally as important as its length.

It should be twenty-four inches wider than the mattress. This allows five to seven inches for take-up on each side, depending on the thickness of the mattress.

For your convenience some sheets are marked with index tabs fastened to the narrow bottom hem of the sheet, indicating whether they are single, three-quarter or double sizes. (See chart on page 123 for recommended sizes of sheets, blankets, blanket covers, etc.)

Fitted sheets are made to fit standard-size mattresses, and measurements must be taken accurately for buying efficiency. The fitted top sheets are mitered at the foot end only and are tailored to stay snugly in place. The top sheets may substitute for bottom sheets also. Though fitted sheets are a trifle more expensive than regular sheets, they are a great convenience and timesaver to busy housekeepers. The fitted bottom sheets can be used satisfactorily without ironing since they are stretched taut. This feature can be a saving to your sheets because ironing is wearing on them.

what are your preferences?

The basis for your linen closet is the traditional white sheet. You can buy these with plain, hemstitched, or scalloped hems, and you will probably want to consider monograms.

Machine-made monograms are less expensive than the hand-embroidered, of course. Specially designed monograms naturally would be hand-done. Monograms are appropriate on either white or colored sheets. Your linen shop will have many examples of monograms to show you and will be able to advise you on them.

With all the glorious colors there are in sheets and blankets, you can include them as an integral part of your decorating scheme. Even though you may not know exactly what your bedroom colors will be, you will be able to find artistic patterns in pastels that will blend with any other pastels you wish to use. Take a flower-sprigged sheet, for example. With it you could use white or a solid color for the bottom sheet, and the printed one for the top. You'll find exciting colors and designs also in stripes, polkadots, plain-colored borders and other choices.

pillows and pillowcases

Pillowcases are made to match all qualities of sheets, and the ideal size is at least two inches wider than the pillow to allow expansion of the pillow when in use. The standard size feather-bed pillow is 21 by 27 inches. The correct size case to use is 45 by 36 inches in muslin and 45 by 38½ in percale. (Domestic-line cases carry measurements by girth of pillow.) Irish-linen standard cases are marked 22 by 36 inches. Standard foam-rubber pillows come in a size 18 by 24 inches and require pillowcases of 38 by 35 in muslin and 38 by 36 in percale.

The softest pillows are filled with white goose down. A firmer combination is down and feathers, or foam latex. Test a down pillow by placing it in the palm of your hand. A pillow filled with *new* down will stay firm while one filled with *old* down has a tendency to droop on the sides.

You'll want to consult your fiancé (or husband) before buying pillows in order to know his preferences. He may like

Examples of Monograms

WITH THREE LETTERS

WITH ONE LETTER

a soft pillow best, a medium hard or a very firm one. Or he may be allergic to feathers and prefer a foam rubber. So be sure to satisfy him on this important item.

minimum requirements in sheets and pillowcases

A satisfactory sheet supply can be figured on the basis of six sheets for each bed. This allows for:

> 2 sheets in use
> 2 sheets in the laundry
> 2 in reserve

For pillowcases figure on three cases for each pillow. For the two of you this means six cases—two in use, two in the laundry, two in the linen closet.

It is desirable to have more of both sheets and pillowcases if you can afford them, for the larger the supply the longer *all* will last. In case of illness, unexpected guests or emergencies, it is good housekeeping to have an extra quantity. Buy a sheet or two as you go along, from time to time, so that you'll avoid having to replenish the supply all at once. Watch the good linen sales which are featured twice a year, for there are many excellent buys offered at such times.

care of sheets

Rotate the household supply so that the same sheets are not used twice in succession. This allows the fibers to dry out thoroughly. Always place newly laundered sheets on the bottom of the pile to insure rotation.

Sheets should be changed at least once a week. Habits and preferences guide a housekeeper as to whether to change both sheets on the bed or one. Some put the top sheet on the bottom and a clean one on top. It may be done weekly or twice a week. There is no fixed rule beyond that of clean sheets.

Mend sheets, if they need it, before washing. This is important to prevent the tear from growing larger. If sheets become stained from medicines, cosmetics, etc., stains should be removed before regular washing.

If you launder sheets yourself, follow directions that come with the sheets. Colored sheets usually have special directions.

Folded sheets should be stored flat in a linen closet, on a shelf, in a chest of drawers, or any place free from dust. Keep them from contact with polishes, medicines, disinfectants.

It is important to check over your bedsprings to be sure there aren't any rough edges which might tear the sheets.

Before stripping the bed, loosen edges of the sheets. Careless yanking to remove sheets from the bed may tear or split them.

Shift the creases in sheets by varying the folds each time. Use a center crease one time, then fold into thirds another time. Creases should be folded into sheets, never ironed.

mattress covers

Besides making your bed more comfortable, a cover for your

mattress and a bed pad will save both mattress and sheets. The pads usually are made of quilted cotton with elastic bands at each corner to keep them from slipping. Mattress covers are of muslin with zippers or buttons at each corner.

blankets

The next bed covering to consider, after sheets, are blankets. There are many types from which to choose and almost any color you could want, either in plain tones or in plaids, checks, or stripes. Striped ribbon bindings, pert multicolored chintz, or satin bindings in the same color as the blanket—all are smart. All-white and ivory-toned blankets are often selected by brides who haven't chosen their bedroom colors, yet want to be certain that all colors will blend.

For warmth and light weight there's nothing like a 100 per cent woolen blanket, and with proper care it should last many, many years.

There are certain terms used in connection with wool with which you will want to become familiar for better buymanship. *Virgin wool,* or *new wool,* means wool that has never been used. Fiber that has been reworked or reclaimed from yarn may be wool but is not virgin or new wool. *Reprocessed wool* has been made up into merchandise but has never been used by the consumer. *Re-used wool* has been used and has been reduced again to a fibrous state and remade into merchandise. By requirement all merchandise is labeled accordingly.

Many different grades of new, reprocessed and re-used wool are woven into blankets, and there are good and poor qualities in each. A good wool blanket is always soft and resilient, since it is made of long elastic wool fibers which are woven evenly and firmly into the blanket. A poor wool blanket is harsh and unyielding to the touch.

cotton and rayon in blankets

Cotton blankets are ideal for summer use, for warm climates, or wherever a minimum amount of warmth is needed. When they are new cotton blankets will retain the heat, but after laundering the nap becomes crushed and needs to be brushed up gently to restore the air spaces which insulate the blanket. Cotton shrinks less than wool, and is less of an investment.

A wide variety of colors is offered in these summer-weight blankets. There are pastels with flower patterns sprinkled throughout, stripes of all widths and colors, and allover designs.

Cotton is also combined with wool for blankets which are marked "part wool." To be warmer than an all-cotton blanket, it must contain at least twenty-five per cent wool. The mixture of cotton in woolen blankets reduces the price, aids in preventing excess shrinkage and even increases the durability without lessening the warmth to any great extent.

Rayon combined with wool, or with cotton and wool, gives a lustrous appearance to a blanket and keeps the price tag low. The most usual combination you will find in blankets of this type is either eighty-eight per cent rayon and twelve per cent wool, or twenty-five per cent wool, fifty per cent rayon and twenty-five per cent cotton.

There are other so-called "miracle fibers" which are constantly being perfected and making their appearance in blankets. These blankets should all be considered as most of them are moth-resistant, offer great resilience and are easier to launder than wool.

for your shopping information

Blankets should measure at least twelve inches longer and twenty inches wider than the mattress. Some blankets are fitted at the foot for easy tuck-in and have zippers at the corners which permit the blanket to open flat for storing.

The nap of a blanket may be long, medium, or short in length, according to the manufacturing process used. A machine containing fine wire points fuzzes up the fibers on both sides of the blanket to produce the nap. In testing for durability, pull at the nap gently. If it is poorly done, the nap will pull out easily. A good nap holds firmly to the blanket fabric. Too much napping decreases the strength of a blanket by weakening the yarns. Examine a lightweight blanket by holding it up to the light to discern whether there are any thin places evident from overnapping. For a heavier blanket push aside the nap and examine the yarns beneath for firmness.

Weight is important to some extent in judging the durability and the warmth of a blanket. The fiber weight of each blanket is usually given in pounds on the label. When weight is evaluated in ounces per square yard you can easily compare weight for the given area, and compare it with others of the same size.

Take note of the bindings of the blankets you are considering. Rayon satin, rayon taffeta, or cotton are customarily used for the bindings and should be of good quality, closely woven. Cotton sateen, which is popular for use on less luxurious blankets, is prone to pick up soil more quickly than rayon bindings, which have a slick surface. From two to four rows of stitching should secure the bindings and be placed a little over the blanket's edge in order that bindings may not shrink more than the blanket in laundering. Lock-stitched edges, with ends firmly overcast, are usual for the finishing of quality blankets. There should be at least seven stitches per inch. Ends that are merely hemmed are practical only on lightweight blankets.

Many blankets are treated to moth resistance, and this claim generally can be trusted, if the label clearly states the type of treatment given and the time limitations expected. Inquire about this feature when comparing merchandise for best buys.

electric blankets and sheets

If you prefer only one bed covering, consider the electric blanket with its assured all-night-long warmth. The electric blanket has enclosed within the major part of it an electric heating element that is made of flexible wires, especially insulated, and is both waterproof and flame resistant. The fabric may be of wool, wool and cotton, or a combination of rayon, wool and cotton. Most brands of electric blankets come in about six colors and have both dual and single controls. Some are fitted at the foot, too.

Single control maintains even warmth over the entire bed.

With dual controls warmth is maintained independently on each half of the bed. If the temperature drops several degrees during the night, the control will automatically provide the heat needed for comfort.

There are also electric sheets which are covered with mercerized broadcloth in pastel colors. The electric sheet is put on over the regular sheet; then a blanket, quilt, or comforter is placed over the top to keep you cozy regardless of the room temperature. It, too, has both single and dual controls.

Whatever you buy in electrical bed coverings, make sure that it has been approved by the Underwriters' Laboratories, Inc., and is labeled so.

Follow the manufacturer's directions carefully as to cleaning and general care. Turn off the current when not in use and always avoid bunching or creasing the cover while the current is on.

care of blankets

Follow directions that come with new blankets. Woolen blankets should never be soaked, rubbed, or washed in hot water. Mild soap or detergent in warm water and a gentle squeezing of the blanket will remove soil and keep shrinkage to a minimum. Soiled bindings may be cleaned with a soft brush dipped in suds. If a blanket is washed in an electric or power washer, three minutes of gentle action is sufficient. Woolen blankets should not be washed in an automatic washer which does not have a selective control. Three minutes is the maximum washing time.

Blankets should be rinsed through several changes of warm

water. Soap left in blankets weakens the fibers and mildew may develop. If possible, a blanket should be hung across several clotheslines and dried in the shade. After it is dry use a stiff brush to raise the nap. The binding should be dampened and pressed with a warm iron.

Blankets should always be washed or dry-cleaned before storing. Pack them loosely in boxes, giving them good moth protection—a liberal amount of naphthalene or paradichloro-benzene crystals scattered among the folds. Wrap the boxes in heavy paper and seal edges to make them airtight.

blanket covers

Blanket covers will save your blankets much wear and tear, besides cutting down on the laundry and dressing up your bed attractively. The covers come in a variety of styles and materials. They should be purchased in the same measurements as your blankets and if long enough, they may also double as summer spreads. Nylon plissé is a popular material that does not have to be ironed. There are also cotton plissé, rayon crepe, challis, etc. Some are tailored with a monogram; some have contrasting bindings in chintz or eyelet embroidery. If you have all-white blankets, you may carry out any color scheme you wish by changing the blanket covers.

bedspreads

The selection of bedspreads probably will not concern you at the time you are selecting your trousseau linens, since it falls into the category of "home furnishings" from a decorating angle. There is a vast array of styles awaiting you, however, whenever you are ready to buy. You will find colorful throws with matching or contrasting dust ruffles, tailored types in faille, taffeta, or satin, and for plain practicality a host of woven cottons, chenille and other fabrics.

comforters

There's nothing quite so luxurious as a down-filled comforter, which provides warmth with practically no weight at all. The down-filled kind is the most desirable and most expensive, but other insulations are available at lower costs. They include feathers, wool, and Aralac fibers. Cotton and rayon also are used as fillings but are heavy and not satisfactory for the purpose.

The comforter cover should be of a good fabric that is closely woven to prevent filling from coming through and pliable enough to stay in place on the bed. Quilted comforters are considered among the most satisfactory types, though they are generally the most expensive—especially if hand-quilted.

Be sure that the size is adequate when buying a comforter. It should be ten inches longer and eighteen inches wider than the bed. Standard sizes range from sixty to seventy-two and eighty-inch widths and seventy-eight to eighty-four and ninety-inch lengths. These are "cut sizes," *i.e.* the way the cloth measured before the filling was put in and sewed. Thick filling and elaborate stitching designs take up the size of the comforter from four to six inches in both length and width.

To test the resiliency of a comforter, press it firmly in your hands and check the quickness with which it rebounds to its

Sizes of Sheets and Blankets for Various Bed Types

TYPE	APPROXIMATE MATTRESS SIZE	SUGGESTED SHEET SIZE	SUGGESTED BLANKET SIZE
Sofa beds, studio beds, etc.	30″ x 75″ 34″ x 75″	54″ x 90″ or 63″ x 108″	64″ x 80″
Single bed	36″ x 75″	63″ x 108″ or 72″ x 108″	64″ x 80″
Twin regular bed	39″ x 75″*	63″ x 108″ or 72″ x 108″	72″ x 90″
Twin long bed	39″ x 90″	72″ x 108″ or 72″ x 113″	72″ x 90″
King-size twin bed	42″ x 80″	72″ x 108″ or 72″ x 113″	72″ x 90″
Three-quarter size bed	48″ x 75″	72″ x 108″ or 72″ x 113″	72″ x 90″
Double bed	52″ x 75″*	81″ x 108″ or 90″ x 108″	72″ x 90″ or 80″ x 90″
Double sofa bed	54″ x 75″	90″ x 108″	80″ x 90″
Double long bed	54″ x 80″	90″ x 108″ or 90″ x 117″	80″ x 90″
King-size double bed	60″ x 80″*	108″ x 122½″	90″ x 108″
Two twin 3/3 beds attached to one headboard, 78″ x 75″ or 80″ require extra-size bedding when made as one bed		108″ x 122½″	90″ x 108″

* Fitted-style sheet comes in this size.

original state. If it does not quickly spring back into shape when new, it cannot be expected to later—and is not a good buy.

It is not practical to try to wash a comforter in average circumstances, but wiser to have it dry-cleaned.

summary of your bedroom linen needs

For your bedroom you will need the following basic items, to be added to as you wish:

> 12 sheets for twin beds
> 6 sheets for double bed
> 12 pillowcases
> 2 pillows
> 2 winter blankets per bed
>   or 1 blanket, 1 comforter per bed
>   or 1 electric blanket per bed
> 2 summer blankets per bed
> 1 mattress pad per bed
> 1 mattress cover per bed
> 1 blanket cover per bed
> 1 bedspread per bed

Bathroom Linens

Terry towels are the most popular of bathroom towels and are to be found in almost any size, color, quality, pattern and price. It's not known exactly when the first ones were made, but there is evidence in the museums that cloth with a terry weave was used by the ancient Egyptians.

The first machine-made towels of terry cloth were introduced in England about 1848. An Englishman had found some material of terry weave in Turkey, brought it back to England and had a machine made to produce it. The terry towels were not popular in England, however, and were shipped to Turkey where they were used for wear as turbans. Several years later importers from England brought them back and sold them as "Turkish" towels.

A mill in Paterson, New Jersey, produced the first American-made terry towels about 1870. They were not accepted in the United States, however, until World War I. Before 1917 the plain weave huck towels were popular, but during the war they were needed in such quantity for the fighting forces that the public was forced to turn to terry towels. After that they became the preferred ones because of their softness and absorbency.

The early towels were plain white or white with colored borders. When color began to play such an important role in household accessories, around 1928, colored terry towels were introduced. Since then improvements have been made in color and design so that towels now are a basic part in the decorative scheme of your bathroom.

Most bath towels are made of cotton since it is easily laundered and is soft and absorbent. Some towels have linen or a combination of linen and cotton loops to produce a harsh texture which suits those who prefer a rough towel. Rayon is used sometimes but is not too satisfactory since it becomes weak when wet. It is usually found in decorative towels and will be recognized by its lustrous appearance.

The quality of the yarn used in towels is important. Good absorbency is assured when the yarn is soft, evenly spun, well-bleached cotton with a minimum of twist. If an inferior grade is used, the towel is apt to be weak, the pile will mat after laundering and it will be stiff and harsh to the touch.

The function of a towel is to absorb moisture from the skin and it must be able to withstand the strain of pulling and tugging, and also survive the wear and tear of frequent laundering.

The surface loops or pile of a terry towel do the drying. Each loop is like a small sponge; when the towel touches wet skin the loops absorb the moisture. The ground weave is the backbone of the towel, bears the load and provides the real strength of terry fabric.

variations in terry cloth

Terry towels are available plain, banded, figured, or printed. The entire surface of the towel may be covered with loops or they may be arranged in ribs or textured patterns. The variations in plain terry are known as dobby, Jacquard, Mitcheline, athletic-ribbed and texture weaves.

Dobby patterns are so-called because they are made on a dobby machine, or power loom, which has automatic mechanisms for shedding warp threads for moderately complicated patterns. The designs usually are small and run parallel to both the length and width of the towel.

Jacquard designs are manufactured on the Jacquard loom which weaves cloth of highly complicated patterns by means of perforated cards much like the rolls used in player pianos. Most towels of elaborate patterns are products of the Jacquard loom.

Mitcheline is the name of a weave, frequently made on a Jacquard loom, where the border designs are accentuated through the use of heavy roving yarns.

Athletic-ribbed towels have alternative stripes of terry and of plain weave running lengthwise of the toweling to give a ribbed effect. This offers greater friction qualities to the towel.

Texture weaves include towels in which an allover pattern or design is made with raised and depressed areas. They are usually woven either on the dobby or the Jacquard loom.

what to look for in buying towels

The underweave of a terry towel is the best indicator of its wearing qualities. The lengthwise and crosswise threads should be firm, close and tight so as to hold the loops securely. Hold the towel up to the light. If only tiny pinholes of light come through, it is closely woven. If light comes through in patches, the cloth is too loosely woven to withstand long wear. Also look at the plain woven stripes or borders. If they are close and firm, you can expect the towel to be durable.

Feel the towel in your hand and compare different weights and grades. You'll notice the difference between sturdy towels with body and those with looser weave, lighter weight. The ones with a firm, close weave will give longer wear. Look for close, thick loops for quick drying. The longer the loops the greater the drying capacity of a towel.

Another important point of wear in towels is the selvage. There are various types of selvage: a fast selvage which is closely woven, an overedged selvage which has stitching closely locked, and a hemmed selvage. Any of these, properly made, give satisfactory wear.

Look at the hems. They should be sewn with small, close stitches, finished with backstitches at corners to prevent ripping.

Towels may feel soft, medium soft, rough and hard. It's all a matter of preference which you choose. Soft towels are more luxurious and are usually favored by women. Towels of medium softness may be preferred by some. Those who enjoy a brisk rubdown may want to have towels of hard or rough texture.

Depend on a reliable brand name or the advice of a reputable store. Some stores carry towels under their own names.

color in towels

Color and design in towels naturally add to the cost and attractiveness but don't necessarily contribute to their efficiency. Lines or bands of color cost slightly more, but solid colors increase considerably the cost of manufacture. Elaborate floral, scroll patterns are the most expensive since they must be woven on Jacquard looms. All-white towels are the most absorbent and least expensive in the same quality as the colored ones. Pastel shades are next and the deep colors are least absorbent of all.

sizes in towels

There are many sizes of towels from the big beach towels to tiny finger-tip ones. The larger bath towels are preferred by many. Most men are partial to the largest size.

Extra-large-size bath towel: 24" x 46" to 25" x 48"
Standard-size bath towel: 22" x 24"
Small size: 16" x 26" to 18" x 36"
Finger-tip size: 11" x 18"
Beach size: 35" x 70" to 36" x 72"

Many prefer to buy their towels in matched sets which consist of bath towel, face-hand towel, washcloth and bath mat. These may match in color and design or you may mix contrasting sets. For example, you may want to have a plain blue set and co-ordinate it with another set with blue and white stripes. This way there is a variation in design, while the color is constant.

When laundry is paid for by the pound you might remember that the larger, heavier towels will cost more. The medium-size bath towel is easier to handle in a home laundry, and less expensive in a commercial laundry.

face and hand towels

Besides terry, there are also huck towels for the face and hands. These are made of cotton, linen and cotton, or all linen. The pattern is in small squares standing out from the background. There are different qualities, depending on the type of yarn and closeness of weave. Huck towels are available in white and a variety of colors.

Handkerchief linen is also used for guest towels. They do look pretty on the rack but can be used only once and crumple easily. The very small ones are scarcely adequate for drying one's hands.

Damask is used, too, for face and hand towels. These are usually linen, although they are also made of cotton and combinations of either rayon or linen.

monograms on towels

Like your other linens for table and bed, towels can be made personally yours with monograms. You may want to carry out the colors of your bed linen in the bathroom with the same type of monogram. You might select your favorite two colors and have the monograms contrast on each—for example, on yellow towels have a gray monogram, on gray have yellow. Then you could carry the colors further in stripes, checks for variety. You might choose one primary color and use the palest to the deepest tone, in blue, for instance, with the monograms contrasting. You'll have many styles in monograms from which to choose and your linen shop will be able to advise you properly on them. Always be careful that your initials don't spell a word! (See samples of monograms on page 113.)

dish towels

Dish towels are now so perky and attractive in design that

they're really conversation pieces for your kitchen. Some are so decorative that they can be used as place mats, or hung up as café curtains. It's really great fun to shop for them.

Dish towels are made of all linen, linen with cotton, all cotton, or combinations of cotton, linen and spun rayon. You'll find that all-linen towels do absorb moisture readily, keep their color, dry quickly and do not shed lint. Long-fibered flax makes the best grade of linen towel because it is regular and can be spun evenly into smooth threads. It is comparatively expensive. Short-fibered linen, if it is closely woven, makes durable and less expensive towels.

Cotton towels which are filled with linen have some of the qualities of all linen. They should have at least twenty-five per cent linen if any of the linen characteristics are claimed.

All-cotton towels which are not specially treated will lint, and unless the yarns are loosely spun, the towel will not absorb moisture. Of course, price is the great advantage of cotton over linen. Cotton and linen when combined with spun rayon are supposed to have linenlike qualities, but the price is lower.

When buying dish towels look at the yarn. The most absorbent towels are made of smooth, soft yarns (not too tightly twisted). Always avoid fuzzy yarns because they will shed lint and show poor quality. For general-purpose towels, a coarse open weave is the most absorbent. For use on glass and fine china, where it is important to avoid lint, you may wish a close weave with finer threads.

Always look at the label when you buy dish towels to check any special claims made by the manufacturer. Always buy colors that are guaranteed fast.

how much do you need?

To start out, the following list should be adequate for bathroom and kitchen for a family of two. Add to the supply as you can, so that you won't need to replace them all at once. Since washcloths get more wear, it is wise to buy some extra ones in your chosen colors.

For your bathroom

12 large-size bath towels
12 small towels
12 matching wash cloths or more
 6 hand towels
 6 guest towels (terry finger-tip or linen)
 2 bath mats
 2 bathroom rugs
 1 shower curtain

For your kitchen

6 hand towels
9 linen dish towels for glass, china
9 dish towels of cotton and linen or other
    combinations
6 dish cloths
6 pot holders

care of towels

Terry towels should not be allowed to become too soiled

and should be washed often. General laundering does not hurt them, but it is harmful to allow grime and dirt to be ground into towels since hard rubbing or chemicals are required to get them clean.

Terry towels should either be hung outdoors to dry or fluff-dried in an automatic drier. If towels are laundered by a commercial laundry, ask to have them fluff-dried and not run through a mangle. Towels are never ironed since that would flatten the loops and lessen the absorbency.

Deep-tone towels should always be laundered separately with a mild soap and warm water. Since a large amount of dye is used to produce the dark tone, it frequently colors the water when towels are washed.

As with your sheets and pillowcases, store newly laundered towels at the bottom of the pile, so that the pile is rotated and the towels get even wear.

Towels never should be used for removing make-up. Always have cleansing tissues available for that. Also special cloths should be provided for razor blades so the men do not use towels for this purpose.

Dish towels should be kept clean and fresh and washed often in hot water with plenty of suds and if possible hung in the sun to dry.

CHAPTER VI

MECHANICAL HELPERS

ONE OF THE PRINCIPAL KEYS TO YOUR EFFICIENCY IN KEEP-ing house will be the mechanical equipment which you can call to your aid for "easy doing." There's a wondrous array of mechanical wizards with push-button controls, from which you will want to select a "basic kitchen trousseau."

First thoughts naturally will turn to *small appliances,* since many of them will be listed among your treasured wedding gifts, and also among your own "first buys," if you are moving into an apartment where the major appliances are furnished.

Your groom should be your main stand-by in helping choose

these long-term investments, for he'll doubtless be sharing the fun of using most of them. And, like most males, he's probably a better judge of mechanical gadgets than you are.

A few appliances carefully chosen is a sound way to start. Often these mechanical aids are not employed to their full potentialities and only take up valued storage space. So make your selections according to estimated usage in all cases, and with a calculating eye toward honest-to-goodness practicability.

In small quarters, particularly, appliances that do double-duty and save time and energy are a real blessing to busy young couples.

Here are a few pointers to consider before beginning your study of the various aids in which you are interested:

1. Make it a rule to invest only in well-known brand-name merchandise, and be sure to specify the desired brand when you register for small appliances on your wedding-gift preference list.

2. If possible, buy locally (in the city in which you are to reside) so that your service guarantee will mean real follow-up service. Consider the consequences before "buying wholesale," as it may mean having to forego the customary free maintenance service granted by the retail dealers.

3. Check carefully on the guarantee made by the manufacturer regarding the machine, and on the replacement of any defective parts. There are variations in manufacturers' guarantees which may influence you to select one brand over another. Always look for the Underwriters' Laboratories, Inc., seal of approval on any appliance. This is essential for your protection.

4. Request a demonstration of the appliance you are considering, and try it out yourself whenever possible.

5. Make notes as you go of the amount of current, in terms of watts, that each of your appliances will consume. Then check the total figure against the electrical load limit specified for your new quarters, in order not to overload the circuits. The solution may be to use continuous strip outlets around the baseboard which can be plugged into at many points.

6. Check the safety features of the individual controls on the equipment you are considering, their readability and ease of operation. If there are children about, the controls should not be within reach of tiny tots.

7. Examine the device for ease of cleaning, and if any parts require separate handling in cleaning, note their accessibility. Make sure that the appliance in question will not take up more time than it saves.

8. Seek out all the information you possibly can on each appliance before you go shopping. Familiarize yourself with "what to look for," and "the evaluations for usefulness," as stressed in the pages following. Then make your selections with confidence and appreciation for the enjoyment in service which each device is bound to bring.

Automatic Toasters

Most young couples consider an electric toaster a requisite to modern marriage, and list it among the very first "gifts wanted" on their preference lists for wedding presents. There are several variations to be found in the different models, and you should designate the make you prefer.

Don't decide on any one type until you have checked the salient features of each to your satisfaction, after studying the following pointers. You will find the mechanism in today's electric toasters simple and dependable, ready to give many years of service without repair.

types available

Most electric toasters are the oven or well type, which holds two slices of bread and toasts both sides of each slice simultaneously.

In the completely automatic toaster the toast pops up when it is done. Other types have audible signals to indicate when the toast is brown.

features to consider

Controls: The majority of toasters have range controls from "light" to "dark," with some models having as many as six positions of control. Many have thermostatic controls, or a combination of the two. With a good thermostatic control the difference in moisture content of bread is compensated so that the toast has uniform dryness. On some of the models toast can be reheated if the control is turned to the lightest point.

Safety Factors: The bottom of the toaster should be well insulated, with a smooth base to prevent table damage. Handles and control knobs should be heatproof.

Performance: The toaster should operate quietly and toast quickly, with no preheating necessary. It should accommodate a variety of bread sizes. Some models are designed with extra-high toast lifts for frozen waffles, small pieces of toast, and even muffins. Heating elements should be of flat metal ribbon or mica sheets for long and even wear.

Talking Points: The finish should be nontarnishable. The toaster should have a hinged or removable crumb tray which opens at the push of a button for easy cleaning. Some have extra-large, snap-out, snap-in crumb trays. In certain models the weight of the bread, as it is put in, lowers it to start the toasting cycle. A combination clock and thermostat control that is automatic assures perfect browning at every setting, regardless of fluctuation which may take place in the voltage.

care of toaster

Empty the crumb tray every few days. Wipe the outside with a damp cloth. Never wrap the cord around the toaster when it is hot. Care should be used not to bang or shake the toaster so that the heating element becomes loose. If small bread slices have to be removed with a fork, disconnect the toaster first to avoid shock.

Never try to clean the interior heating element, as it is self-cleaning when current is turned on. A small brush is useful to remove crumbs, if the toaster has no crumb tray.

Automatic Coffeemakers

If you are coffee lovers, you'll find the automatic electric coffeemaker a real joy. The fact that you merely fill it, plug it in, take a shower and dress and find the coffee done to your taste is certainly a timesaver in the morning. It's so easy to make good coffee with these automatic coffeemakers. Whether you're dining alone or entertaining a crowd, you'll always get the same result—good coffee.

types available

There are two kinds of automatic coffeemakers: the *vacuum* and the *percolator*.

In the *vacuum* coffeemaker water is heated in the lower bowl; steam forces it up into the top section where the coffee grounds are. It stays there and agitates vigorously until the current shuts off automatically; then it filters back to the bottom container, as the steam pressure lowers.

In the *percolator* a small amount of boiling water rises up a narrow tube and sprays over the coffee grounds in the basket. It drips through the grounds and returns to the bottom where it continues this process of boiling up and over the grounds until it reaches the desired strength.

features to consider

Controls: In the completely automatic coffeemaker there is a two-heat unit which automatically switches from high to low heat after coffee is brewed and keeps it at that serving temperature while it is plugged in. On most percolators a red signal light goes on to indicate that the coffee is ready to serve. On the vacuum type the coffee is done when it returns to the lower bowl and the switch automatically moves to "low" to keep it hot.

Safety Factors: Heatproof handles and bases are essential for easy handling and for table protection. Some are footed and others have a flat, heatproof base.

Performance: The percolator is a trifle easier to operate since coffee is ready to pour as soon as it's done. With the vacuum type the top bowl which contains the grounds must be removed before coffee is poured. In the vacuum, too, there's a filter of cloth or glass or stainless steel. The glass and stainless steel ones are easiest to clean.

Sizes in automatic percolators vary from four cups to ten cups. The eight-cup size is a popular choice. In some as little as two cups can be brewed at a time; others have a minimum of three or four. In some vacuum models as little as one cup can be brewed, even though the actual capacity is eight or ten cups.

Each new model brings out improvements—to speed the brewing, to vary the strength, to make small or large amounts of coffee—so be sure to follow the manufacturer's instructions to achieve best results.

Talking Points: Most coffeemakers have fill marks, are easy to assemble and to clean. Vacuum brewers should have wide mouths for easy cleaning and nondrip spouts. On percolators there is usually a dial indicating "Mild," "Medium," or "Strong" to set to insure brewing just the way you like it.

The finish should be nontarnishable. Most of the automatic coffeemakers have a chrome finish over copper, aluminum, stainless steel, or brass; others are of heavy polished aluminum.

care of automatic coffeemaker

Clean thoroughly after each use. The inside of the pot or bowls should be kept very clean for the best coffee flavor. Never assemble or cover the pot until it has been allowed to air and dry. Be sure that the base of the coffeemaker is never immersed in water since that would injure the heating element. Always rinse well. It's a good idea to put baking soda and water in the pot occasionally and proceed as if you were making coffee. This cleaning method applies to all except aluminum pots which have their own special cleaner. Never connect the coffeemaker before water is added nor leave it connected after it is empty.

Electric Mixers

If your hungry half is blessed with a sweet tooth and you have a yen for cake baking, you'll doubtless want an electric mixer as a kitchen helper.

There are many other uses to which you can put a mixer, too. It beats almost everything and will save you much manual labor, besides cutting down the time necessary in hand beating.

From the delicate mixing of an angel-food cake to the sturdier work of chopping nuts and cutting raisins, you'll find an electric mixer (and its adjuncts) handy and dependable. If your kitchen is small and storage space limited, you may want to settle for a portable model, made to hang on the kitchen wall.

These are some of the electric mixer's most common uses:

whipping cream	mixing dough and batters
beating eggs	beating candy
mashing potatoes	chopping and creaming eggs
mashing cooked fruit	blending sandwich mixes
puréeing cooked vegetables	mixing icings
creaming butter and cheese	mixing puddings

types available

Some electric mixers are permanently attached to a base. Others are on a base but have detachable mixing units and juice-extractor attachments.

Portable models have only beaters and motors without a base. They are adequate for most kinds of mixing, such as mashing potatoes, mixing icings, etc. Portables are lightweight, can save space by hanging on the wall, and are usually capable of several speeds.

features to consider

Controls: Most mixers have multispeed controls, and the control dials should be easy to read and to operate. The mixer motor should have adequate speed for all mixing jobs (with the exception of a portable model), and should give constant speed at any setting, even with the heaviest of batters. Motors with radio-interference eliminators and sealed-in lubrication are desirable.

Safety Factors: The base of the mixer should be well balanced to prevent tipping. Beaters should be easy to insert and there should be an ejector for easy removal. The two pyrex bowls which usually come with the mixer set are more serviceable and less likely to slip from the hand when made with ribbed surfaces, rather than a smooth finish.

Performance: The mixer should perform speedily and not spatter during its operation. Beaters designed to pull the batter into their circulating blades are recommended. Off-center beaters which allow maximum pouring space are a desirable feature. Turntable action should be reliable, and the mixer should perform reasonably quickly.

Attachments: Most food mixers come equipped with several attachments, such as a juice extractor, meat chopper and shredder, along with the beaters. These attachments may be top-mounted or side-mounted. They should be easy to attach, easy to use, easy to clean. Be sure that the motor is strong enough to accommodate all the attachments, as most of them require more power than for mixing operations.

Talking Points: Look for a model with a lightweight, easy-to-detach mixing unit for convenient portable use at other work surfaces (if you are concentrating on the larger mixer). An easy-to-attach, easy-to-clean juicer is a convenience. Check the length of attached cord to make sure it permits ample radius for working.

Make certain your mixer carries a guarantee for a period of one year from date of purchase, and that the manufacturer will replace any parts that may prove defective within that period.

care of mixer

Before using the mixer, see that the turntable has been adjusted so that the beaters just touch the bottom of the bowl. Handle bowls with care, and avoid sudden temperature changes to prevent cracking. After each use wash the beaters and bowls, and wipe the entire appliance with a damp cloth. Keep the mixer covered when not in use, and for convenience's sake, store it where it is ready for instant attachment and use.

ELECTRIC BLENDERS

You may well consider this one of your most important appliances, if all its accomplishments fit your daily menus.

A blender will do much more than mix drinks and liquefy solid foods. It takes all the drudgery out of grating, chopping, mincing and shredding, and whips and mixes foods in a few seconds. It is a drink mixer's joy, and useful too for mixing canapé dips and spreads. And the way soups, sauces, beverages and salad dressings come out of the blender smoother than silk in consistency seems almost a miracle, impossible to achieve by hand.

While an electric mixer is ideal for taking care of large amounts of food to be creamed or beaten together, the blender gives its best results when working with small amounts at a time—making it especially adaptable in cooking for two.

Blender blades will clog if an overload of food is crammed into it. Also, it is not satisfactory for beating egg whites, mashing potatoes, or crushing ice, and must be watched very closely when whipping cream because of the super-fast action of its stainless-steel blades.

Here are some of the *unusual* feats a blender can accomplish:

> Chops onions without tears
> Makes applesauce without peeling apples
> Makes a sherbet or frappé from a mixture of fruit,
>   juice and crushed ice
> Takes the curdle out of hollandaise, the lumps out of
>   gravies
> Mixes a cake, waffles, pancakes and quick breads from
>   prepared mixes in twenty seconds
> Grinds coffee, when manufacturer's instructions are
>   carefully followed

Heed the instruction booklets which usually contain many recipes, and as you use your blender you will find many more services for it to perform.

types available

All blenders are basically alike, with a motor enclosed in the base and a covered container equipped with stainless-steel blades which revolve and do the cutting, chopping, or mixing.

Some containers have line markings at four, eight, sixteen, twenty-four and thirty-two-ounce levels to give exact measurements for recipe following. One model has a two-piece top with a removable center for adding ingredients without splashing while the blender is in operation.

features to consider

Controls: Most blenders have two or three speeds. All have fast whirlwind action which varies in speed according to the amount and type of food being mixed.

Safety Factors: It is essential that the machine you select be made with a base heavy enough to stay firmly placed on the table or counter while in operation. Test the model you are considering to see that it does not tip easily.

Performance: The containers of most blenders have tops of heat-resistant glass which are tempered for making hot drinks. Metal containers for making exceedingly cold drinks are available in another model, principally for bar use. Most homemakers prefer the glass-style container so that they may watch the food as it is being mixed.

Some blenders are noisy and interfere with radio and television, while others are equipped with a radio-interference eliminator.

Talking Points: A blender which comes apart at the base of the container, so that the parts may be washed separately, is a great convenience.

The machines which are designed with a threaded base to permit a Mason jar to be screwed into place instead of the regular container offer advantages also. This feature makes it possible to prepare salad dressings, sauces and spreads in pint or half-pint jars, to be stored away in the same jars.

The blender container varies in capacity in various models, so buy one that best suits your family needs. Remember that it should never be filled beyond two thirds of its capacity.

Blender bases are available in different finishes, ranging from an enamel finish (the least costly) to shiny, nontarnishable chrome. Select a blender that you will like looking at as well as using, then keep it attached on your kitchen counter, ready for instant use.

care of blender

The glass container of your blender will wash itself if you toss some soap flakes or detergent into it along with a little warm water, place the lid on and turn the switch. Or you may wash it with a bottle brush in your dishpan. Rinse and dry with care. Do not subject the container to sudden extreme temperature changes by letting cold and hot water from the faucet run directly on it. Where cutting blades are removable the cleaning job is a cinch.

Wipe off the base of the blender with a damp cloth after each use. Most machines do not need home oiling, but you had best consult the blender booklet which comes with the appliance for full instructions on perpetual care.

WAFFLE IRONS

If waffles appear regularly on your breakfast or snack menus, an automatic electric waffle iron might well be a favorite servant. But if you yearn for them only about once a year, there's no use in crowding your shelves with a waffle iron. Frozen waffles can be easily prepared in your electric toaster for occasional servings.

types available

Waffle irons are available in a variety of shapes: round, oval, square, rectangular. Some square ones have an extra-large baking area that makes four waffles at one baking. Twin waffle irons make two good-sized waffles at one time.

features to consider

Controls: Automatic irons have signal lights to indicate when the waffles are done. Some have a dial for setting the baker for the desired degree of brownness. Nonautomatic irons have an indicator which shows when the grids have reached the baking temperature, but the baking time must be watched. Opening the grids before the waffle is completely cooked often will ruin the waffle.

Safety Factors: The bottom should be smooth and well insulated to protect the table, and handles should be heatproof.

Performance: Follow the instructions carefully in regard to preheating the grids and as to the amount of batter which should be poured on the grids. Time the baking if the appliance is not an automatic, and you should always have waffles done to the right golden crispness. Recipe books usually accompany the book of instructions.

Talking Points: To allow waffles to rise while baking, there should be expansion hinges, preferably enclosed for easy cleaning. Baking grids should be made of solid cast aluminum, and the outer finish should be nontarnishable chrome plate. The base should be broad enough to catch excess batter, if there is not an overflow trough.

care of waffle iron

Most waffle irons have been pretreated at the factory, but if not, this should be done by brushing with salad oil or unused fat. Heat iron to the smoking point, pour on batter, bake and discard the first waffle.

After each use wipe grids with a damp cloth, polish with a dry one. Never immerse your waffle iron in water as this would ruin the heating unit. If grids were silicone treated at the factory (instructions will tell you), wipe with a damp cloth and never use a wire brush.

Always preheat according to instructions. When baking is finished, disconnect immediately and open grids to cool before cleaning.

Keep the finish bright by washing with a soft cloth in warm soapy water. Polish with a dry one.

COMBINATION SANDWICH GRILL AND WAFFLE IRON

For late-hour snacks, impromptu lunches, or for short-order cooking of chops, hamburgers, etc., the combination sandwich grill and waffle iron is a happy choice of appliances. Since it is versatile, it could very well be one that you'd use practically every day.

As a grill, it fries bacon, scrambled eggs, French toast, ham, cooks hot toasted sandwiches, or grills chops, frankfurters, hamburgers. For making waffles, the waffle grids are easily inserted and clipped in place.

types available

The combination grill and waffle iron is usually either square or oblong. Heating units are in both the cover and the bottom surfaces. The automatic has temperature control dial and indicator light. The nonautomatic has everything but these two features.

features to consider

Controls: The automatic has a temperature control for baking waffles to your taste (degree of brownness), and an indicator light which glows when the waffles are done. For the grill, some models have a light that shows when proper temperature has been reached; on others the light goes out when preheating time is reached. Follow the manufacturer's instructions carefully.

Safety Factors: Handles and control knobs should be heat-proof. A hinged handle on the cover unit forms a firm leg when flat grids are being used for grilling. Some manufacturers advise putting an insulating pad under the combination grill and waffle maker when using it on a polished wooden or linoleum table top or on a tablecloth.

Performance: When used as a grill, the appliance is opened flat so that food—bacon, eggs, hamburgers, chops, etc. —may be cooked on both surfaces. When grilling sandwiches, the upper grid is closed over the sandwiches for toasting. To make waffles, the waffle grids are inserted and clipped in place. The words "upper" and "lower" are usually marked near the edge of the grid for easy identification.

Talking Points: Look for extra-large drip spouts so that the excess grease from frying or grilling is drained away easily. Use a small cup to catch drippings. Some models have permanently seasoned waffle grids with grooved edges to prevent overflow. The interchangeable waffle grids should lift in and out quickly and simply. Look for grids that have been treated to give even distribution of heat over their entire surface and that heat quickly.

The finish should be nontarnishable. Most of the models are chrome-plated.

care of sandwich grill and waffle iron

Keep finish bright by washing with a soft cloth and warm soapy water after each use. Polish with a soft dry cloth.

After cooking on the grill, wipe grids while slightly warm with a paper towel or damp cloth. If grids are stained from certain foods, cool completely, remove, wash in soapy water. Dry thoroughly and season again before using. (After continued use grids may darken, but this does not mean they must be washed.)

Always leave sandwich grids open to cool after use. This prevents the fat used for seasoning from burning off.

Never place the entire grill in water as this would injure the heating unit.

When waffle grids have been used, cool completely with the grids open. While warm, wipe with a soft cloth or absorbent paper. If washing is necessary, remove the grids, wash with soapy water and a bristle brush. Rinse and dry thoroughly. If scouring powder is used, be sure to rinse it completely from the grids.

ELECTRIC BROILERS

There are any number of electric broilers on the market, and all are especially adapted to small-apartment dwellers, who have limited cooking equipment and not-too-efficient stove broilers.

A special advantage of the electric broiler is that you don't have to bend over to manipulate it, as with most stove broilers. It does heat up the kitchen somewhat, but not so much as some stoves do (more, however, than an electric roaster). In tiny kitchens heat is felt from almost any type of appliance. The broilers also spatter a bit, particularly when broiling chops that have much fat on them, so a spatter guard is a wise thing to have.

With an electric broiler you may broil almost anything that you can broil in a stove, and do it better. This process improves the flavor of most meats, imparting a charcoal taste, but it does not make the meat any more tender than other types of broiling.

types available

There is the closed, dome-shaped broiler with one rack which prevents hot grease from spattering out into working surfaces.

There is the open-front, box-shaped broiler with adjustable racks which often has a grill on top for warming or cooking. The open front allows for closer cooking observation, and is generally more convenient to use.

features to consider

Controls: There is more than one degree of heat on most broilers. The selection usually includes medium, high, and full; or low and high.

Safety Factors: It's important to know the amount of heat the broiler radiates in order to avoid injuring the table top on which it is to be used. Handles and plugs should be heatproof for easy handling.

Performance: A broiler that requires preheating takes a few minutes longer to prepare for use than one which needs no preheating. Usually the open-front, box-shaped type does not require this preheating. For satisfactorily cooking rare and medium meats, broiling time should be fast. Generally speaking, the broilers that don't require preheating cook more quickly.

Talking Points: In the open-front type there should be several rack positions. More than one kind of food can be prepared at one time, particularly if there's a grill on top.

care of broiler

Clean the racks, base, and pan or trays with soap and water and a mild cleanser, if necessary. Wipe chromium finish, after cooling, with a damp cloth; polish with a dry one. Do not immerse the broiler in water.

ROTISSERIE BROILERS

Although this is rather expensive equipment, the rotisserie broiler is a favorite appliance, particularly with the man of the house. It can do anything a broiler can do, plus roasting meat, fowl and fish, and barbecuing. A rotisserie has a revolving motor-driven spit for barbecuing and roasting. Most models have a broiler tray and a grill tray.

features to consider

Controls: Many models have three heats—high for broiling and grilling, medium for roasting or barbecuing, low for keeping foods hot. Some have an automatic "stay-away-all-day" timer which starts and stops automatically.

Safety Factors: Most rotisserie broilers are of nontarnishable material that's easy to clean. Heatproof handles and corners are necessary. A spatter shield with an oven-glass window prevents grease from spattering and you can see the food as it cooks. This shield also helps the broiler retain moisture so that roasts cannot dry out. A concealed rotisserie motor with separate switch is desirable.

Performance: The rotisserie broiler gives a delicious outdoor charcoal flavor to food. It may be used round the clock in the kitchen, dining room, porch or outdoors. Most models are portable. Some have large cooking areas which permit preparing an entire meal all at one time. You can barbecue and roast turkeys, prime ribs of beef, whole hams, chickens, loin of pork, leg of lamb, wild fowl and game; or broil steaks, chops, fish, ribs, bacon, Shish Kabobs, etc.

Talking Points: Those appliances that have the infrared coils covering the entire broiling and grilling area cook faster. Double-wall construction retains heat for quicker and better cooking. In some models adjustable tray racks are removable for simple cleaning, and afford a larger area for broiling.

care of rotisserie broiler

All the removable parts of a rotisserie broiler, such as racks and trays, should be washed thoroughly after each use. The inside of the broiler should be wiped carefully with a damp cloth; otherwise grease will accumulate, harden, and be difficult to remove. If there are sharp edges where the side panels are attached, be sure to wear gloves when wiping it out to avoid finger damage. Some models have nicely rounded corners. Check on all advantageous points when buying one.

ELECTRIC ROASTERS

These miracle helpers are portable, can be plugged in anywhere, and will do almost any kind of cooking. They roast, bake, stew, or steam. They can also broil, toast and fry with the addition of a broiler-griddle attachment.

An entire meal may be cooked without any surveillance necessary. The roaster clock can be set to start automatically any time you wish; you may be gone for hours, then return to find a completely cooked meal.

For couples living in small apartments with inadequate kitchen ranges an electric roaster is a gem. It is also a boon to the working wife who may fix dinner before she leaves in the morning and find it ready to serve when she comes home in the evening.

types available

Electric roasters come in rectangular and oval shapes. They are compact in build and are available in various sizes. The outer frame of the appliance is usually made of welded steel, finished with baked acid-resistant enamel.

The small-sized roasters which may be placed on the dining table for both cooking and serving have completely automatic heat control.

The average size has a capacity for roasting up to nine pounds of meat. The largest size can accommodate up to twenty-four pounds. The liquid capacity of the roasters ranges from six to twenty quarts.

features to consider

Controls: Thermostatic controls regulate the heat of all models. Some have adjustable vents which govern the amount of moisture retained within the roaster.

Safety Factors: The roaster should be convenient to carry. The lid and insert pans should be easy to maneuver, and of easy-to-care-for materials. Usually they are made of aluminum, plated brass, or a stainless metal alloy.
Certain models have automatic cover lifters, which eliminate touching a hot cover at any time. Most machines have cool plastic dials and handles for carrying.

Performance: Many of the models have a cooking well, with inset pans that are designed for easy removal and smaller cooking dishes made of heatproof glass, porcelain enamel, china or aluminum.
Some of the smaller roasters combine the advantages of a casserole, deep-well cooker, baker and small roaster.

Talking Points: For special convenience some of these modern wonders are made with adjustable shelves, making it possible to bake pies and cakes on two levels while meat is roasting in the cooking well.

A glass observation window is the added feature of one model, which also has a self-basting roaster cover, where steam from cooking condenses and drops back to baste the food. Special insulation in some of the small roasters makes it practical for carrying to picnics or to potluck suppers, with the food holding its heat for hours in the serving pans.

A built-in clock is an asset in a roaster.

care of roaster

Wipe roaster with a damp cloth after using. Never immerse the outer portion in water when cleaning. Always detach the broiler unit from the griddle before cleaning.

DEEP-FAT FRYERS

If you are fond of French-fried shrimps, potatoes and vegetables, you will find the electric deep-fat fryer a happy choice in appliances. The quick-frying process is excellent, but the fryers necessarily require a rather large quantity of fat, which, however, may be used over and over again with success.

types available

The deep-fat fryers come in saucepan style, round and square shapes, and a number of them are designed in toaster form.

Many are combination cookers and fryers which are quite versatile in that they simmer and cook such foods as soups, stews, cereals, sauces, gravies, puddings, and will also deep-fry anything from chicken to doughnuts.

Designs in the combination types range from flared bowls to chafing-dish styles, all handy for table serving as well as cooking.

features to consider

Controls: All styles have temperature control dials and signal lights to indicate when the correct cooking temperature is reached. Some models have lighted cooking guides or charts conveniently placed on the front of the appliance, which list the best temperature settings for simmering, cooking and frying foods used most often.

Safety Factors: The cooker base in most models is equipped with a heat shield to give lower table-top temperature. Drain spouts for removing frying fats are safety features.

Talking Points: Lightweight spun-aluminum fry baskets for deep frying are easily cleaned and very durable. Some combination appliances have bowls of chrome-plated steel, with cast aluminum cooking wells. Certain shapes of the deep-fat fryers require less fat for cooking than others. As a gauge, for instance, one six-quart capacity cooker calls for three pounds of shortening for all normal frying.

Another model has extra-large capacity; it will fry up to three pounds of quartered chicken.

Some fryers can serve also as steamers, bun warmers and corn poppers.

care of deep-fat fryer

Even though there is a drain spout on some models to remove the fat, it is quite a cleaning task to keep these fryers in shining order.

Wash the wire basket and cooking pan in warm soapsuds. Wipe off the baked-enamel base with a damp cloth. Never immerse the base, or cooking well, in water.

ELECTRIC SKILLETS

Skillets have been completely glamourized as exemplified in automatic electric models. They can be plugged in anywhere and guarantee correct, automatically controlled heat for good cooking and frying without constant watching.

types available

There are both round and square models of the automatic electric skillet. Some have high-dome covers which can be bought separately; others have flat covers included with the skillet.

features to consider

Controls: In some the heat control is in the handle where the dial can be set for bacon, eggs, hamburgers, chicken, etc., so that the foods will be cooked to perfection automatically. In others the heat control indicator is on the side of the pan.

Safety Factors: Sturdy heatproof legs and handle make it possible to use the skillet almost any place.

Performance: Its many uses include cake baking, chicken frying, popping corn, as well as stewing, roasting and frying. Even distribution of heat eliminates hot spots and provides an even, over-all temperature. It can be regulated to keep food at serving temperature after it is cooked.

Talking Points: Automatic heat control removes the guesswork from cooking since anything from scrambled eggs to steaks can be cooked at the correct degree in the electric skillet. Some models have a water-sealed heating element so that for cleaning the entire pan may be immersed in water up to the control knob. The square shape provides a little more cooking area. This type of cooking results in less grease absorption in foods than in stove cooking since the shortening remains constantly at the right temperature.

care of electric skillet

If the manufacturer's instructions state that the pan may be immersed in water, it can be cleaned in that way. Otherwise use soapy water to clean the inside of the pan and merely wipe the outside with a damp cloth.

Electric Knife Sharpeners

With an electric knife sharpener only a few seconds are required to put a keen edge on any knife blade from kitchen knives to the finest carving set.

features to consider

Controls: A guard guide holds the knives at the correct angle so there's no danger of the knife slipping. On some models the guard guide is removable for sharpening scissors and other tools.

Safety Factor: If too much pressure is used, the sharpener stops automatically.

Talking Points: Look for the kind that sharpens all types of blades—stainless, vanadium, or hollow-ground steel. Some models are rubber mounted at the base; others have suction cups to prevent sliding on the table while knives are being sharpened.

care of knife sharpener

Plastic cases are easy to keep clean—just wipe off with a damp cloth or use soap and water. Don't immerse it in water. Most of the electric knife sharpeners have fan-cooled motors that don't need oiling.

AUTOMATIC ELECTRIC IRONS

Automatic irons are a very popular item on gift-preference lists, wedding counselors report. And since most young home-makers have had very little experience in shopping for this particular appliance, a study of the various types available will prove valuable in making the best selection possible for your specific needs.

The old theory that an iron has to be heavy to perform its function well has been exploded. Ironing has become a much easier task now with the lightweight, automatic electric iron, built with a sensitive thermostat to keep temperatures controlled for ironing any fabric with safety.

features to consider

Controls: The controls on an iron should be legibly marked and easy to move. A fabric dial is the best type to have because various fabrics require different temperatures. The simple, easy-to-read dial is usually marked "rayon," "silk," "wool," "cotton," "linen." This is preferable to a marking of "low," "medium," "high." Some models also have an "off" position indicated on the dial so that the iron may be turned off without disconnecting the cord.

Safety Factors: The cord should be at least six feet long, heavily insulated, and with a guard at the point of attachment. There should be a comfortable heel rest. The heel rest is preferable to a side rest and less tiring, since it requires no lifting of the iron. Some models have a wrinkleproof heel, which is desirable. The heel rest, handle and temperature control knob should stay cool.

Performance: The lightweight automatic iron saves energy since it requires no bearing down for good results. With thermostatic control it is safe for all fabrics. Always read instructions for ironing synthetic fabrics, set the dial to the desired temperature and the thermostat will provide the protection.

Talking Points: Handles should be shaped to fit the hand. Some have thumb rests. There are also open-handle models which keep the wrist relaxed for efficient manipulation, and make pocket ironing a breeze. Beveled edges or special niches for ironing buttons are assets. The point should be sharply shaped for easy ironing of ruffles, etc. An iron that is pointed at both ends can be used for either hand. Or if there is a reversible cord, you can iron left-handed or right-handed with facility.

An iron should weigh from three to four pounds and have a wattage of about 1,000. Soleplates (the bottom of the iron) vary in size from twenty-one to twenty-nine and one half square inches. A very satisfactory size is twenty-five inches.

Try out the iron for size, if you can. Test it for easy handling and for quick and even heating.

care of automatic electric iron

Keep the bottom of the iron clean. Wipe off with a damp cloth while barely warm. If starch sticks, rub the iron lightly over waxed paper while it is slightly warm. Never immerse an iron in water. If necessary, use soapsuds or mild scouring powder to remove stains. Disconnect the iron from the outlet by grasping the plug itself—never jerk the cord. Do not store an iron away until it is cold. Never wrap the cord around a hot iron.

Nonautomatic Irons

There are also nonautomatic irons which are cheaper than the automatic types, but not nearly so efficient. They supply heat without thermostatic control, or they may have a simple heat-limiting device which shuts off the current at a maximum temperature for safety.

features to consider

Controls: Most models have temperature controls for various fabrics, but the irons must be disconnected in order to reduce the heat.

Safety Factors: The iron should come with a separate stand on which to rest it for safeguarding against burning the ironing board.

Performance: Since the temperatures have to be kept comparatively low for safety, this iron depends on its weight for ironing efficiency, and usually weighs about six pounds.

care of nonautomatic iron

Follow the same instructions given for the automatic iron.

STEAM IRONS

Most steam irons are a combination steam and dry iron. They eliminate the need for dampening clothes and speed up the ironing process. They are particularly helpful for someone who doesn't know very much about ironing, since it's practically impossible to do a poor job.

types available

There are two types of combination steam and dry irons. The kettle type produces steam by bringing water to a boil, much in the same way a teakettle does. (See sketch.) The flash-boiler type makes instantaneous steam, with water dropping onto a heated plate, drop by drop. This type is usually preferred since it produces only one drop of steam at a time. (See sketch.) There are also some dry-iron models which come equipped with steam attachments that fit on the back

part of the iron. They perform the same function as the regular steam iron but are more bulky in appearance.

The Steam Iron

FLASHBOILER TYPE   **KETTLE TYPE**

features to consider

Controls: Make sure the steam iron has thermostatic heat control. Some models also have a control to regulate the
steam. With some irons the steam stops automatically
when placed on the heel rest and starts again when
the iron is picked up. This saves the steam in case you
are called away while ironing.

There should be a fabric dial. A combination iron
that is designed for good dry ironing will usually
have dependable heat control for steam ironing.

Safety Factors: The iron should be designed for easy filling
and emptying. Special care should be exercised when
emptying the kettle type. Those that are filled from
the front part of the handle seem easiest to empty.

Performance: You can iron almost any fabric without danger, even though a pressing cloth is not used, if the material is pressed on the wrong side. It is best to sprinkle heavy, starched cottons and linens before ironing with the steam iron. Light fabrics do not need to be dampened.

Talking Points: A combination steam and dry iron can do all household ironing effortlessly if it can be converted quickly and easily. A steam iron should be lightweight and easy to handle. Weights vary from three to four pounds, the majority weighing about three and one half pounds when empty. The capacity should be about one cup of water which, in a good steam iron, gives forty-five minutes of ironing time.

It should be easy to switch from dry ironing to steam ironing, or vice versa. It may be by the mere click of a switch. Or in some models the iron has to be emptied after steam ironing, before it is ready to dry iron. If that's the case, arrange to do your dry ironing first.

care of steam iron

Distilled or rain water is best for use in a steam iron when tap water is quite hard. Melted frost from your refrigerator may be used as a substitute.

When your ironing is completed, the water remaining in the iron should be emptied and the cap left off until the iron has had a chance to dry inside.

For cleaning, it is a good idea to pour a solution of equal parts of vinegar and water into the tank about twice a year and let it heat until steam appears. Then pour out and rinse with clean water.

As in the automatic iron keep the bottom of the iron clean by wiping off with a damp cloth.

GENERAL CARE OF ELECTRICAL APPLIANCES

1. Never connect an appliance to a lamp socket; always use an outlet.

2. If the cord is not attached, insert the appliance connection first, then plug into the outlet.

3. Always disconnect an appliance for cleaning or repairing.

4. Allow a heated appliance to cool before storing it.

5. Never yank at a cord. Remove it from the outlet by grasping the plug.

6. Repair or replace a cord at first signs of wear.

7. Do not place cords under rugs or in places where they may be pinched, or where their insulation is likely to wear off.

suggestions from young marrieds

After surveying the field of small appliances, you may be in a bit of a quandary about which ones to choose for your start in life. Perhaps you feel you must limit your choices to three or four, and you're wondering which ones will work best for you, now and later.

To check into this very question, we asked a number of young marrieds to list the three small appliances they have found the most indispensable for their manner of living. Here are a few of the answers which may help guide you in your selections.

One newly married couple lives in an apartment hotel, where full service in linens and housekeeping is furnished. The kitchen is postage-stamp size, little more than a serving pantry. The career-girl wife, however, likes to whip up a meal now and then, and to serve occasional breakfasts (with instant-type coffee). The three favorite appliances for their style of living happen to be:

1. *An automatic toaster* for toast, waffles and muffins, which serves them well not only for breakfasts but also for brunch on Sundays, late snacks and teatime foods.

2. *An electric broiler* for cooking steaks and chops faster and better than the little kitchen-range broiler does. It also keeps the kitchen cooler. Sometimes on summer week ends the broiler goes outdoors on the terrace for a cooking spree, and for special fun.

3. *An electric blender,* which happened to be a gift not of their own choosing, but now rates high as an indispensable for making salad dressings, soups and desserts. Its most frequent uses include mixing frozen orange juice for breakfast every morning (makes it nice and frothy), and for whipping cream for desserts in twenty seconds flat (no need for a failure when you stand guard).

Another couple interviewed has an airy four-room apartment with a fair-sized kitchen, reliable stove, adequate storage space. As wedding gifts they received almost every type of appliance made. The ones they value the most and keep working constantly are:

1. *the automatic coffeemaker*
2. *toaster*
3. *combination steam and dry iron*

Their portable mixer also got high rating as a fourth choice, and they recommend trying to wangle one as a gift, if possible. Theirs hangs in a convenient spot on the kitchen wall, handy to an electric outlet, and always ready for action.

Especially is their combination iron a "rave" with this housewife, who is clever at making things on her electric sewing machine and swears she couldn't get along without this efficiency aid for pressing draperies, slip covers, suits which she tailors, etc. It's a timesaver too for ironing hubby's shirts, with no dampening necessary.

We asked another happy pair, who entertain quite a bit, just how they rated their electrical appliances, and here's how:

1. Number One on their list is the *rotisserie broiler*—their pride and joy for adding dash to their cocktail and buffet parties. Perched in a place of honor on the counter bar of their dining alcove when they entertain, this impressive appliance keeps turning out hot hors d'oeuvres before the very eyes of their guests and keeps everyone drooling for more.

2. Their next-in-line favorite electrical gadget, both members of this household agree, is their big double-bed *electric blanket* with its twin controls, which they consider a necessary luxury when the winter winds blow.

3. Number Three billing was given to their *combination sandwich grill and waffle iron*, which they declare is "kept cookin'" almost constantly over the week ends for casual breakfasts and brunches, evening suppers and late snacks,

when they bring it right to the table for easy performance.

"We'd love a houseful of electrical wonders if we could have them," this couple declares, "but as long as there are some limitations, we'll take the more spectacular appliances for ours—and make coffee in an old-fashioned pot and toast in the oven, if we have to."

CHAPTER VII

KITCHEN NECESSITIES

FROM THE FIRST DAY YOU TAKE OVER A DAILY ROUTINE OF kitchen duty, you owe it to yourself to have the necessary equipment. The right utensils and proper organization in your kitchen may mean the difference between pleasure and drudgery. And there's no excuse for the latter with all the wonderful double-duty, timesaving tools there are available.

As with your wedding planning, you should take time and study your culinary needs before buying even so much as a measuring spoon. The size of your kitchen is a first consideration. If it is exceptionally small, you'll have to decide on the bare essentials, concentrating on those items that can serve many purposes and which are convenient to store and easy to care for.

A double boiler, for instance, converts into two saucepans. One deep skillet with a lid serves as a frying pan, chicken fryer, a Dutch oven. Or a heatproof glass pan may be used as a baking dish, too.

In buying kitchen utensils it is important to invest in good quality, since well-made pots and pans, knives, etc., will serve you a lifetime.

Consider these basic characteristics of quality before buying:

1. *Durability:* The material should resist warping, bending out of shape, chipping and breaking.

2. *Cooking efficiency:* Heat should be transferred evenly and quickly, and should be retained. The material should not be affected by acids, grease or food alkalies.

3. *Cleaning ease:* Utensils which are smooth, have few parts, and are stain-resistant are easiest to clean.

4. *Easy to use:* Handles and knobs should be heatproof and convenient to grasp. Covers should fit snugly. The inside finish should be treated to prevent excessive sticking.

5. *Easy to store:* Choose utensils with nesting abilities, or those that are easy to hang.

6. *Safe to use:* Handles that do not turn when used are found on the best-quality merchandise. Vents, gauges, safe closures (on pressure cookers) and spouts should be designed for safety to the user.

sizes and shapes of utensils

Pans for cooking on top of the stove should cover the heating unit. Bottoms should be flat. Straight-sided utensils conduct heat faster than those with flared sides and require less space on the stove. Covers should be close-fitting to retain steam.

Double-lipped pans are easy for both right- and left-handed persons. A small, round lip causes spilling. A large lip with a sharp point is safer and easier to use.

Utensils must be well-balanced, the handles comfortably long, securely attached and heat resistant.

Frying pans that are easy to handle but heavy enough to withstand warping from heat should be your choices. Saucepans and baking utensils may be lighter weight, since they are used with medium heat.

Oven pans are made of metal, pottery or glass. They should be designed for easy handling with pot holders. Be sure that the pans fit into your oven. A large pan should allow plenty of room for circulation of air around it. If the pans touch the side of the oven, the baked food may be browned where the pan touches.

Pressure cookers are made in various saucepan sizes. The makes differ in the materials used, the methods of closing and controlling pressure, and in the kinds of pressure-indicating devices. It is wise to investigate the different choices available before deciding on what will best meet your needs and be easiest to use. After buying, always follow the manufacturer's directions carefully for use and care.

materials used

The cooking efficiency of each type of material is determined by its ability to utilize heat. In general, lightweight utensils heat rapidly but lose heat quickly and are best for muffin tins and cooky sheets. Heavier utensils heat less rapidly but hold the heat longer.

Aluminum: Like silver, aluminum is too soft to be used alone, and is usually combined with a small percentage of other metals for kitchenware. Aluminum utensils distribute heat quickly and evenly and are strong and durable. Sheet aluminum is made in different gauges or thicknesses. Pans made of this are usually light and smooth with a satiny finish inside and out. Those of a medium or heavy gauge are the more durable. Those from light gauges are suitable for oven use but not for the top of the stove.

Cast aluminum is thick and heavy and used for top-of-stove utensils. A good quality resists pitting and staining. It should be stored uncovered.

Inside stains on aluminum utensils may be removed by using a good powdered aluminum cleanser or steel wool. Household acids such as vinegar, lemon juice, cream of tartar may be used to brighten darkened areas. The darkening of aluminum has no harmful effect on foods, according to the United States Department of Agriculture. If salty water is used or moist food left standing in an aluminum utensil, pitting may occur.

Stainless steel: This is a comparatively expensive alloy which combines nickel and chromium with steel. It's almost indestructible. It will not rust, is resistant to stain and corrosion, the finish will not wear off and it is easy to clean. It heats slowly, however, and conducts heat unevenly so that pans made entirely of this metal tend to become too hot in spots and will scorch food unless heat is kept low.

The best utensils have aluminum or copper applied to the bottom to distribute the heat evenly. So when you see a stainless-steel pan that is aluminum-clad or copper-clad, you can be sure it will give excellent service.

Stainless steel is easily cleaned with soap and water. The finest steel wool or gritless cleansing powder may be used to remove stubborn spots. Overheating may cause dark spots which cannot be removed, but the usefulness of the pan is not harmed.

Copper: There are few utensils made entirely of copper because of its costliness and the difficulty in keeping it bright and shiny. Copper is an excellent heat conductor and as such is often applied to the bottoms of pans made of other materials. Since copper oxide, developed during the cooking process, may be injurious to health over a period of time, all-copper cooking utensils must be lined, usually with tin or stainless steel. Copper pots give the best service if they aren't polished. A powder made especially for cleaning and polishing copper is available, however, and may be used.

Heatproof glass: Glass utensils have many advantages, such as not absorbing moisture or odors and not being affected by acid or alkaline foods. But they also have the disadvantage of being breakable.

There are two types of glass utensils:

1. Ovenware, which is not to be used over direct heat
2. Top-of-stove glass (Sometimes called flameproof or flameware.)

Glass should always be used over moderate heat and should never be allowed to boil dry. Avoid sudden changes in temperature which cause cracking or breaking of glass utensils. It is advisable to use an asbestos pad under top-of-stove utensils. Fine cleaning powder is recommended for use on glass utensils. In removing stuck or burned food from glass, soak it in soda water for easy riddance. Fine steel wool may be used to remove stubborn spots.

Enameled ware: This is made by fusing glass onto a steel base by firing at high temperatures. It is smooth, nonporous and easy to clean. Its quality depends on the number of coats of enamel and thickness of the base. Inexpensive enameled ware is dipped only once in gray or dark-blue enamel and is often called graniteware. Medium-priced enameled ware is dipped twice, the most expensive three times. Most manufacturers indicate on the label whether the utensil is double- or triple-coated.

While enameled ware has a glasslike surface, it is more fragile than metal and may chip or crack with careless handling, sudden knocks, or changes in temperature. It has to be cared for as glass.

Soak stuck foods before washing. Don't use coarse scouring powders or metal pads, as they will scratch. When stirring food in an enameled container, always use a wooden spoon to avoid scratching. Enameled utensils are used mostly for top-of-stove cooking and in the oven for roasters, as they tend to overbrown baked goods.

Cast iron: Utensils made of cast iron are hard and thick and good for long, slow cooking. It's a favorite material for Dutch ovens and frying pans, but large pans are too heavy for easy handling. Some cast-iron utensils are seasoned by the manufacturer and are ready to use; others must be seasoned. Check this on the label.

The attractive, enameled cast-iron utensils, which come in bright hues for oven-to-table ware, may be used either in the oven or on top of the stove. They should be cared for as any enameled ware.

Tinware: Tin utensils conduct heat rapidly but do not hold it. When tin pans are new, foods baked in them brown only slightly. When the surface darkens with use, heat is absorbed more rapidly and food is baked to an even brown. Tinware is not suitable for top-of-stove utensils. It should always be washed and dried well; it should not be scoured or scraped with sharp tools. Cheap grades may have pin-point holes in the tin coating, which can't be seen until rust appears.

Ceramic ware: Heat-resistant ceramic utensils are colorful and attractive, and suitable for baking dishes that go right to the table. Ceramics are cleaned easily by soaking and washing and should be protected from sudden temperature changes. Avoid putting hot dishes in cold water or even on a cold table top.

cutlery

Cutlery should be chosen for the various tasks it is to perform. Good cutlery reduces the time in food preparation.

Poor cutlery is not only a waste of money but a constant annoyance.

The best grade of knives is made from high-carbon steel containing ninety-five points of carbon or more. Knives containing less than eighty points of carbon will not hold their cutting edges.

Since very few cutlery products are labeled, it is necessary to depend on informed salespeople in the cutlery departments to supply the needed information.

Here are basic points to consider:

1. Blades that are tapered from the handle to the point, and from the back to the cutting edge, usually are forged blades made of high-carbon steel of the finest quality. Each blade is processed individually, which makes forged products more expensive than others.

2. Many good medium-priced blades are formed by beveling, a process which cuts out two blades at a time from a bar of metal, thick in the middle and thinner at both sides. These blades taper from back to cutting edge, similar to the forged knives.

3. Blades also are stamped out from metal sheets. They can be counted on to give good service if formed of high-quality alloy steel. Inferior grades of knives, however, are often made by this process and are not satisfactory for long-time wear if inferior materials are used.

4. It is a mistake to try to judge the quality of a knife blade by its flexibility. Whether it is rigid or flexible depends entirely on the purpose it is to perform. Butcher knives and bread knives, for instance, serve best by being firm and rigid. Paring and boning knives, in contrast, serve their purpose best when flexible.

5. In selecting a knife, test the balance of the blade and the feel of it in your hand, to see how comfortable it is to use. If it is a paring knife, do a bit of shadow peeling or paring with it, as you would in actual use.

6. The word "stainless" is stamped on blades which are made both of steel and of iron. The stainless steel, when made of a high-carbon content, will retain a keen cutting edge longer than stainless iron blades, made from an alloy of chromium and iron.

7. Knife handles that wear best are made of metal, rubber, fine-grained woods or synthetic compositions. Polished woods are more satisfactory than stained and varnished wood handles. Paint on handles will chip and peel after a short time.

Your own preferences, chosen from this wide variety of cutlery, should lead to a minimum of at least two paring knives, a general-purpose stiff-blade knife of large size, a carving set and a long flexible slicer, as well as a few special-purpose knives, such as a fruit knife with serrated edges, a cheese knife, etc. Fruit knives are often made of transparent plastic materials, unaffected by food acids, and can be resharpened.

Following is a list of equipment for various-sized kitchens. This can be changed to suit your own needs, but has the basic essentials for beginning housekeeping:

For a small kitchen

Bottle opener
Brushes: vegetable and pastry
Cake pan: shallow, square or oblong, in glass or metal. Can also be used for meat loaf, scalloped dishes, etc.
Can opener

Casseroles: one large and four individual ones
Chopper
Chopping bowl: small, wooden
Cutting board
Dish drainer
Double boiler
Egg beater: rotary
Fork: two-pronged, long handle
Grater
Jar opener
Juice extractor
Ladle
Knives: bread knife, butcher knife, carver, grapefruit knife,
    paring knife, utility knife, vegetable parer
Measuring cups: two—one for liquids, one for dry measure
Mixing bowls: nested
Mixing spoons
Muffin tin
Pancake turner
Pastry blender
Pie pan
Potato masher
Roasting pan: medium size with rack
Saucepans: 1 or 1½ quart and 3-quart with covers
Scraper: rubber
Skewers, set of
Skillets: 5-inch and 10-inch with covers
Spatulas: rubber and metal
Thermometer: meat
Timer, if range doesn't have one
Tongs for lifting hot foods or ice cubes

Wire strainers: medium and small
Wire whisk

For larger quarters add

Cake pans: angel-food cake; three 8-inch or two 9-inch cake
    pans
Canister set
Cheese cutter: wire
Cooky sheet
Custard cups or ramekins
Cutting board (an additional one)
Deep-fat fryer basket
Dutch oven
Egg slicer
Flour sifter
Funnel
Grater set
Griddle
Kitchen shears
Knife sharpener
Measures: pint and quart
Molds
Rack for cooling cake
Refrigerator storage dishes
Roaster: large with rack and cover
Rolling pin
Saucepan: 4-quart with lid
Scales for weighing food
Skillet: 7-inch
Teakettle
Wooden spoons, set of

If among your appliances you don't have an electric coffee-maker, of course you'll need a coffeepot in your list of kitchen equipment. Choose the vacuum or percolator type in metal or heatproof glass.

planned kitchen storage

An organized plan for storage of utensils, pots and pans, dishes and glassware in your kitchen makes work lighter and eliminates fatigue.

If you are building a home of your own, you can, of course, have storage and work surfaces just the way you wish them. But the majority of brides move into rented apartments or houses where the kitchen equipment is already installed and is often inadequate. For storing trays and large platters, you might insert vertical racks. The secret is to store things in a way that they're easy to find and in places near where they'll be used. Hang as many things as you can. Establish work centers.

Food storage and preparation should be near the refrigerator. There you might have such things as knives, can opener, egg beater, measuring spoons, etc.

Near the sink plan storage space for all cleaning supplies and utensils used first with water.

Near the range have utensils which are used in cooking and those used also for the serving of food.

Use the least accessible storage space for items which are used only once in a while. Here we give you two sketches showing the usual arrangements in small kitchens. They are keyed to show the placement of the various items. You will want to vary it, of course, in accordance with your own housing arrangement.

One-Wall Kitchen Arrangement

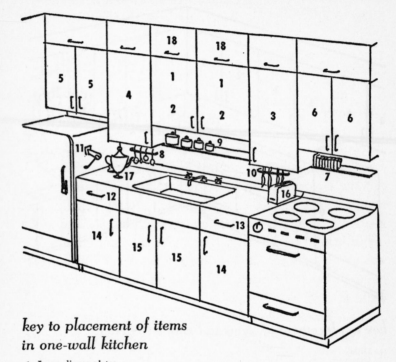

key to placement of items in one-wall kitchen

1. Large dinner plates
2. Smaller china pieces, hooks for hanging cups over them
3. Glassware
4. Staples and frequently used canned goods
5. Storage for canned goods
6. Mixing bowls, refrigerator dishes, molds, etc., occasionally used utensils
7. Herb shelf
8. Magnetized bar for much-used measuring spoons, spatulas, etc.
9. Shelf for canister set
10. Magnetized rack for knives and implements
11. Suction can opener can be put on side of refrigerator
12. Drawer for kitchen forks, spoons, spatulas, egg beater, pastry blender, shears, wire whisk, etc.
13. Drawer for table silver
14. Pans for cake, pie, square ones, loaf ones, skillets, saucepans, roasting pan, cooky sheet, cake racks, trays, any shallow pans
15. Cleaning supplies, wastebasket, household tools, any bulky items. Towel rack inside door
16. Toaster on counter
17. Coffeemaker on counter
18. Curtain wall or space above cabinets can be fixed with hinged doors to store items that are infrequently used

L-Shaped Kitchen Plan

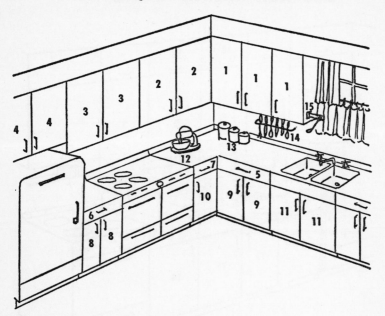

key to placement of items in l-shaped kitchen

1. Dishes
2. Glassware
3. Staples and everyday provisions. Cabinet fitted with step shelves for herbs, spices and condiments
4. Storage for canned goods
5. Drawer for kitchen implements
6. Drawer for kitchen linens, dish towels, pot holders, aprons, etc.
7. Drawer for table silver
8. Large pans and frequently used appliances
9. Smaller cooking utensils, mixing bowls, refrigerator dishes
10. Vertical racks for trays and shallow pans
11. Under-sink storage, towel rack inside door
12. Electric mixer
13. Canister set
14. Knife rack
15. Can-opener fixture

CHAPTER VIII

PUTTING YOUR TREASURES
TO WORK

THE JOY OF HAVING LOVELY HOUSEHOLD ACCESSORIES, OF course, is in making active use of them in your everyday life. There's no satisfaction in having hidden treasures stashed away in a storage closet, awaiting some special occasion which may never come. They should all be easily accessible and put to frequent use.

Start right by taking inventory of what you have—wedding gifts included—then devise ways of putting everything to work that you possibly can.

If you find yourself with two chafing dishes, don't relegate one to a top shelf. Learn how to synchronize them with a flourish for a "Mr.-and-Mrs." party meal, where your husband makes his meat speciality before the eyes of doting guests, and you concoct the dessert course to follow it. Or if, among your gifts, you have a soup tureen, by all means put it into service in several ways. Use it for oyster stew, onion soup or some such delicacy for Sunday-night supper. If it's large enough, count on it as a punch bowl for holiday occasions, and use it often as a decorative flower container.

If a few odd pieces turn up which don't seem to function

well under their own guise, perhaps you can figure out some other use for them. Oversized trays can sometimes be turned into table tops, extra cocktail shakers made into "planters" for growing plants and a pretty Lazy Susan attractively utilized as a table centerpiece for fruit and flowers.

It is all these accouterments to living that will set the tone of your day-by-day life, as well as your entertaining occasions. If you begin by playing the part of a gracious hostess to your most interested audience (that ever-lovin' man of yours), as a natural role every day, you won't have to put on assumed party manners when your guest list expands.

Once you have acquired your favorite patterns in china, silver, crystal, pretty linens and the necessary equipment to back them up for efficient service, you'll want to show them off to good advantage—not only when your bridesmaids come to luncheon, or your husband's boss comes to dinner, but when just you-two are alone. The secret is to learn how to operate everything correctly—from electric toaster to finger-bowl service—before you start presiding over your household.

Make a study of the various approved ways of doing things, such as setting a table, serving meals sit-down and buffet style, seating guests, etc., then decide on the procedure you want to adopt as yours in the brand-new family traditions you are starting.

table settings complete

There are certain rules of social etiquette and custom that cannot be disregarded in setting a table and serving a meal, and to know the *right way* of doing things is necessary to every hostess. Your table decorations, or centerpiece, depend on your own taste and imagination, but the placement of the table service is dictated by convention and convenience and follows a traditional code.

The three points to consider in planning your table settings include:

1. The table covering
2. The table decoration
3. Each individual place setting

They should be planned in co-ordination, keeping in mind balance of design and color and appropriateness to the occasion.

Here are some basic pointers to follow:

1. Make sure that the background for serving a meal is conducive to enjoyment; that the dining room (or wherever you are serving) is well-ventilated, in tidy order, and that the table is the correct size for the number to be served.

2. Set the table with care (never with a slap-dash attitude) and check to see that each place setting is complete, with every piece in place.

3. Avoid a crowded or cluttered appearance on your table.

4. Consider table-setting not as a chore but as a creative art, employing ingenuity and individuality.

5. See that every piece of silver on your table is as bright and shining as polishing can make it at all times, and that every piece of glass gleams brilliantly. The stricter you are about this point the more inviting and attractive your meals will be, whatever the occasion.

6. Whenever a bare table top is to be used as a background for serving the table should be in excellent condition, with a high polish, and, of course, heat-resistant and marproof.

when a tablecloth is used

If an opaque cloth such as damask or linen is used, a silence cloth of slightly smaller measurements should be laid under it. The tablecloth must hang evenly on all sides and have no creases except the center fold. An overhang of about twelve to fifteen inches is usually considered correct, but the larger the table the longer the drop may be.

Lace cloths, or sheer organdies, fine handkerchief linen and embroidered cutwork cloths are laid directly over the table with no silence cloth. If you use a colored cloth underneath a sheer one, for a special occasion, make certain that it is the same size as the sheer one.

place mat procedure

You don't have to use a tablecloth even for the most formal of meals unless you so choose. Place mats have come to be acceptable now even for really elegant dinners if they are of exceptionally fine quality and design.

A matching center runner is not necessary but may be used if desired, and if the table is wide enough to accommodate it well.

Each place should be marked with a place mat, with the edge of the mat very near the edge of the table.

Place mats should provide sufficient protection against table marring, so that underpads are not needed. Place mats are not suitable to buffet service, as they tend to give a "busy" effect.

seating arrangements

You'll want to experiment with different seating arrangements for various occasions. There are many variations and no set rules where the host and hostess should sit. Convenience is the best guide to follow.

At long rectangular tables a place for one is usually laid at each end of the table with places for guests arranged along each side. Or you may use only one side and two ends of the table for place settings, if your oblong table stands along a wall or is placed at a window with a view.

If it is a very narrow table of refectory style, you may have all the places arranged along the sides. If square, as many as can comfortably be accommodated may be seated at each side of the table.

Allow plenty of elbowroom for each person—about twenty-four to thirty inches is the minimum per person.

Guests of honor are accorded seats directly to the right of the host and hostess. A woman guest of honor is at the right of the host; a man guest of honor sits at the right of the hostess. (See diagram following.)

table decorations

Distinction in your table setting can be accomplished with inexpensive accessories as well as costly ones. It's the clever

Dinner Party for Eight

```
        7      8      2

    3                      1

        4      5      6
```

Guests of honor are always seated to the right of the host and hostess, as indicated. Married couples are not usually seated together. Men and women alternate in the seating, as nearly as possible, if there is an even number.

1. Host
2. Woman guest of honor
3. Hostess
4. Man guest of honor
5. Woman guest
6. Man guest
7. Woman guest
8. Man guest

placing and graceful arranging of a centerpiece which often turns the trick.

Here's where you can let your personality expand. Forget your inhibitions and the usual bowl of flowers in the center of the table, flanked on either side with a candle. Do something out of the ordinary.

Create in your mind what you want to accomplish, carrying out the principles of color harmony, balance and proportion, appropriateness and simplicity. It may be wild flowers in a silver gravy boat, a tray of colorful gourds or scrubbed vegetables, a compote of fruit with ivy intertwined, a many-tiered epergne. Or it could be a figurine with floating blossoms at its base, a parade of blooming plants marching down the center of the table, individual demitasse cups filled with tiny nosegays—whatever your fancy prompts.

When the table is situated in the middle of the room, the decoration usually looks best in the middle of the table, but try experimenting with other positions. At a table for six, for instance, you might have a decorative arrangement at each end of the table, and seat the host and hostess on each side of the table, opposite each other.

If your dining room is small, or you are serving in the living room, consider pushing the table against the wall and placing the decoration at the back of the table.

The centerpiece should be kept small and low for a sit-down dinner with only a few people present. Larger arrangements are appropriate for more formal affairs at long tables.

Candles should be above eye level, from fourteen to sixteen inches high, depending on the holder. Don't stint on candles if you are depending on them for light. At least four candles should be used for serving a table of four.

When you are taking inventory of accessories and their possible uses, make special notes regarding your silver serving dishes which can be utilized as decorative pieces for table centerpieces. Then keep them polished and ready for frequent use, in an accessible place. You might designate a certain closet shelf for nothing but flower containers of all sizes and shapes, figurines, etc., and add to the collection as you see interesting pieces. It will help inspire you with ideas and make it easier to change your scheme of decoration often.

individual place settings

When setting the table for a sit-down dinner, each place is marked with a service or dinner plate. The plates should be placed evenly on both sides of the table, each directly opposite the other about an inch from the edge of the table.

Arrange the silver in order of its use with the tips of the handles in line with the plate and far enough from the edge of the table so they won't brush off easily.

Silver used in the left hand is properly placed on the left of the plate, and that used in the right hand, at the right. The piece to be used first is always on the outside, bringing the silver used last closest to the plate in logical, orderly fashion.

Here's how:

Forks are at the left of the plate, with tines up, in order of use. The seafood fork is the only exception; it is placed at the right of the spoon.

Knives go to the right, with sharp edges toward the plate.

Spoons should be placed to the right of the knife, bowls up, in order of use, beginning outside. When a long-handled iced-tea spoon is used, it goes to the extreme right.

Note: No more than three forks and three knives should be used at each setting. If a menu requires more, bring them in as needed.

Water glasses should be placed slightly above the tips of the dinner knives. If wine or other beverages are added, they go to the right of the water glass. More than three glasses at a place would overbalance the setting and are never used.

The bread-and-butter plate goes to the left of the plate, above the forks. Place the butter knife on the rim of the plate, either vertically or horizontally to the edge of the table. The first wine glass to be used should be placed on the outside within easy reach and should be removed by the time the second is ready for use.

Individual salt and peppers or smoking equipment should be placed at the tops of the service (or dinner) plates. Large salt and pepper containers usually go between every two covers if individual ones are not used.

Dessert silver should be brought in later with the dessert or you may follow the English way of arranging the dessert silver above the dinner (or service) plate, parallel with the table edge. After-dinner coffee spoons, like teaspoons, are placed on the saucers, to the right, under the handle of the cup, when serving.

Napkins are placed at the left of the forks when setting the table. Or for most formal dinners, when the first course is not served until after guests are seated, the napkin is simply folded on the plate. Following are the various ways napkins may be folded.

folding a napkin

Simple foldings of a napkin are always in the best taste. The dinner napkin, which is customarily twenty-two inches square, is folded in thirds and in thirds again. (See Figures 8, 9, 10.) For a soft oblong roll or rectangular folding, the napkin is folded in thirds and then in half. (See Figure 11, 12, 13.) The roll or rectangle should not be longer than the diameter of the service or dinner plate.

The large oblong napkin, or "lapkin," is folded once through the center, then formed into a narrow roll.

If napkins are monogrammed they often require special folding. When the monogram is in the center or in the left-hand corner, the napkin is formed into a soft roll with the monogram uppermost. (See Figures 14, 15, 16.)

Napkins for informal affairs, such as breakfast, buffet supper, luncheon or afternoon tea usually measure from twelve to eighteen inches square. The triangular folding may be used (Figures 6 and 7), with the corners placed away from the plate and the diagonal fold unpressed.

When these smaller napkins bear a monogram, or design, the oblong folding of the quarter-folded napkin may be used. (See Figures 1, 2, 3.) The decorated corner is placed in the lower outside point, to the left of the forks. If the monogram is arranged diagonally in the corner, you may fold as in Figures 4 and 5.

order of table service

When dinner is announced, the hostess leads the way into the dining room, followed by the guests, adult members of the family, children, then the host.

Folding a Napkin

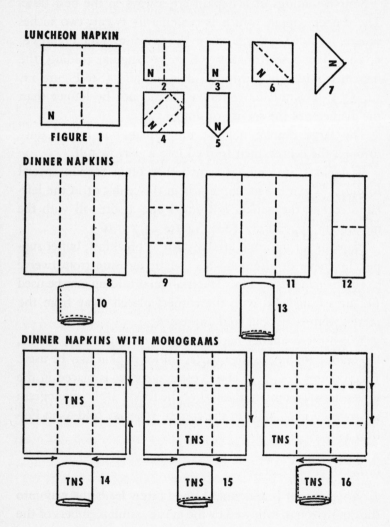

LUNCHEON NAPKIN

FIGURE 1

DINNER NAPKINS

DINNER NAPKINS WITH MONOGRAMS

The hostess may be served first if you choose, though many prefer having the guest of honor served first. Decide what your procedure is to be and inform your husband so that he may follow it when serving the plates at the table.

The service (or dinner-size) plate on which the appetizer or soup course is placed when dinner (or luncheon) is announced is not removed until the main course is served.

Service is always from the left (except for beverages), and removal of plates is from the left. At a strictly formal affair, guests should never be left with a vacant place between courses. When one course is removed it should immediately be replaced with another.

Salad with the main course is placed at the left or directly above the dinner plate. When a hot beverage is served, it should go on the right, just below the water glass.

Hot breads should be folded in a napkin or a linen case especially designed for hot-bread service. Cake or cracker plates may also have doilies.

All silver should be manipulated by the handles. Extra silver may be carried and placed from a small tray.

A glass should never be lifted for refilling, except at very informal meals when the water pitcher is on the table.

At the dessert course, the table is cleared of everything except the centerpiece, ash trays and mint and nut dishes, if any. The meat platter is removed first, then the individual plates, and finally even the salts and peppers. Only the water glass and silver for dessert are left at the individual places.

The table may be crumbed, if necessary, with a folded napkin and a small plate. Metal trays, scrapers, etc., should not be used.

When the finger-bowl service is used, set the finger bowl

on the plate you are using for dessert, with or without a finger-bowl doily. Have each individual bowl one-third full of warm water. A thin slice of lemon may be added, or for extra festive occasions you may want to float a rose petal or two in each bowl. The dessert silver goes on the plate, the dessert fork to the left of the finger bowl, the dessert spoon to the right.

When after-dinner coffee is served at the table, it is placed at the guest's right hand. The spoon is on the saucer. The sugar is passed and cream also if desired.

If the coffee is served after dinner in the living room, the coffee tray may be placed on the coffee table before or after the guests enter the room. The hostess usually pours, placing a lump of sugar on each saucer or informally asking each guest what he prefers. A guest may volunteer to assist the hostess by passing the coffee to the guests.

Procedure for Everyday and Party Occasions

the importance of breakfast

This is the meal that colors your entire day. Whether it's served in a formal dining room, a breakfast alcove or in the kitchen by a window, the setting should be attractive and colorful.

Table Service

It doesn't take much effort to set a tempting breakfast table. Here, you can really play with color and mix or match china to your gayest tablecloths or mats.

Aim for a fresh, scrubbed, uncluttered look, taking the same care in setting your breakfast table that you do for dinner. There should always be some cheery note of decoration: a bowl of fruit, a red geranium, a fresh flower in a bud vase, amusing figurines, or floating blossoms.

If you like a cigarette with that last cup of coffee, be sure to have an ash tray handy, with cigarettes all ready in a little container on the table.

A Morning Timesaver

If time is limited in the morning, with both of you bound for work, why not set the table the night before so that everything is in readiness when you get up in the morning? With your blessed electrical appliances at hand, it takes only a few minutes to get your breakfast under way. The electric toaster, the coffeepot, and the waffle iron, too, can be doing their work at the table while you are having your fruit and cereal courses.

Following is a diagram showing the correct setting for breakfast for two.

The luncheon-size plate is the one to use for breakfast with a bread-and-butter plate, and butter spreader placed on it. The rest of the silver, of course, depends on the menu. On the right of the plate there may be a spoon for fruit, then a cereal spoon, and a luncheon-size knife. The water tumbler goes at the top of the knife, fruit juice next to it or on the plate. When cereal is served, the bowl is usually on the plate to start.

As the hostess, you should serve the coffee, and you'll find it convenient to have a tray at your place on which the coffee-

Breakfast for Two

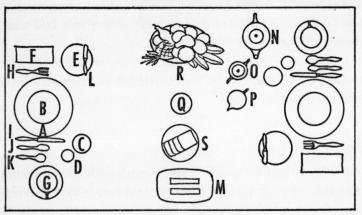

A	Breakfast plate
B	Cereal bowl
C	Water glass at knife point
D	Fruit juice glass
E	Bread and butter plate
F	Napkin
G	Cup and saucer
H	Fork
I	Knife
J	Coffee spoon
K	Cereal spoon
L	Butter knife
M	Toaster
N	Coffeepot
O	Sugar bowl
P	Creamer
Q	Jam or jelly
R	Centerpiece of fruit
S	Plate with toast

pot, sugar bowl, cream pitcher and cups and saucers are placed.

If you have discovered the convenience of little finger bowls at breakfast, they may be placed at the top of the plate, between the bread-and-butter plate and the tumbler. The bowls have a real utilitarian purpose, particularly when there is fruit that requires using the fingers, and buttered toast and jam.

the breakfast tray

You may, on occasion, such as a lazy Saturday morning, relish the idea of having breakfast on a tray in the bedroom or living room. It's also a pleasant way to serve breakfast to a guest and leaves the hostess free to catch up on things in the kitchen. Should someone in your household have a bad case of sniffles, being served a tempting breakfast on a tray is a nice way to be pampered, or to pamper.

When fixing the tray, think of it as a miniature table setting and make it just as attractive. The size of the tray is important, for it should be large enough to contain all the necessary dishes without crowding or tipping, and still be light enough to be handled comfortably.

Use a tray cover of organdy, handkerchief linen, or a combination of materials (with a matching napkin); or one of your prettiest place mats will do nicely.

For the purpose, you should remember to press into service the special little breakfast-tray set which may be one of your wedding gifts. (Or you may have assembled one of your own, when you bought your china.) Such a set is quite complete and usually includes:

Breakfast on a Tray

A	Breakfast plate
B	Fruit juice
C	Water glass
D	Bread-and-butter plate with butter knife
E	Coffee cup and saucer
F	Napkin
G	Fork
H	Knife
I	Coffee spoon
J	Covered toast dish
K	Coffee pot
L	Creamer
M	Sugar bowl
N-O	Salt and pepper
P	Jam or jelly
Q	Flower or nosegay

breakfast plate	cream pitcher
cereal dish	egg cup
cup and saucer	bread-and-butter plate
covered toast dish	salt and peppers
sugar bowl	individual coffeepot

Also ideal for the breakfast tray is the nested coffee service which may have been numbered among your gifts, either in silver or in china. Made in small size, it usually consists of the coffeepot, a small sugar bowl which fits into the top of the coffeepot, a cream pitcher fitting into the top of the sugar bowl and a cover on top of that, which also fits the coffeepot when you dispense with the creamer and sugar.

See diagram showing the placement of dishes and silver on the breakfast tray. Add a flower touch of some sort—a single blossom in a colorful finger bowl, or a tiny nosegay in a miniature vase—and the picture is complete.

luncheon or brunch

If it's a late Sunday-morning breakfast party, you'll probably call it brunch. On any other day it will more regularly be called luncheon. The menu is about the same for both, and the table setting similar. If you are serving buffet style, follow the procedure given later in this chapter.

The table may be colorfully arrayed with place mats, colored damask or a bright linen cloth, organdy, or whatever you wish. Candles should not be used with the centerpiece at noon, generally speaking, unless the room is quite dark.

Luncheon for Four

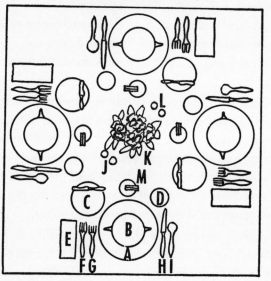

A	Luncheon plate	H	Knife
B	Bouillon cup	I	Bouillon spoon
C	Bread and butter plate with butter knife	J	Salt and pepper
		K	Centerpiece
D	Water glass	L	Another pair of salt and pepper
E	Napkin	
F	Fork	M	Cigarette and ash tray
G	Salad fork		

If fruit cup or melon is the first course, a teaspoon is used instead of the bouillon spoon. If fruit or tomato juice is served, no spoon is needed. The spoon for the beverage is served with it. However, if iced tea or coffee is served during the luncheon this should be set on a coaster or small plate at the right, in the position the cup and saucer would occupy. The beverage spoon would be in the same position as the bouillon spoon above. Wine may be served at luncheon and the wine glass is placed to the right of the water glass, as for dinner.

Use luncheon-size plates in pottery, china or glass (especially attractive for a summer luncheon).

Cream-soup cups and saucers are correct, never soup plates for luncheon unless soup is to be the main course (when you serve from a tureen). If you haven't cream-soup cups, use tea cups. If you lack bouillon spoons, use teaspoons.

Luncheon rarely consists of more than three courses, and usually only two. Even though the menu doesn't require a knife, it should be placed there anyway on the right of the plate, as many use it with their forks for eating all types of foods. If hot coffee is in order, it may be served in the living room just as after-dinner coffee is served. Or it may correctly be served at the table with the hostess pouring. Tea is more often the favorite beverage at luncheon, or iced tea or coffee at a summer luncheon. All of these are served at the table, often with the main course.

See a diagram of a luncheon table correctly set, page 207.

dinner for two

When the two of you are dining alone, the setting should be as gay and charming as if you were entertaining guests. Use a different tablecloth or place mats from the ones you had at breakfast, and dress up the table with your best china, if you have two sets.

Set the table carefully, with all tools needed.

Don't skip the salad fork to save dishwashing.

Use the bread-and-butter plates with butter spreaders, unless you plan to serve rolls already buttered.

Do use candlelight now and then. It's flattering both to you and the food.

Dinner for Two

with host carving and serving

A	Dinner plate	L	Carving knife and fork
B	Soup plate	M	Platter with divisions for meat
C	Bread and butter plate		and vegetables
D	Water glass	N	Serving spoons
E	Wine glass	O	Salad plates
F	Napkin	P	Salad bowl
G	Dinner fork	Q	Salad serving fork
H	Salad fork	R	Salad serving spoon
I	Knife	S	Candlesticks and candles
J	Soup spoon	T	Centerpiece
K	Bread and butter knife	U	Individual salt and pepper

Host serves meat and vegetables. If vegetables are in two separate dishes, they may be placed on his right and left, with the meat platter above as in M in diagram. Carving set can be placed to right of platter, serving spoons above one of the vegetable dishes. Or all the serving implements can be placed in line with the silver on the right of the host's plate.

Hostess serves the salad either as a separate course, or to be eaten with the main course. This can be placed on a near-by table or serving cart if there isn't room at the table.

Encourage your husband to carve at the table, if he doesn't mind, for it is a nice custom to establish, even for two. Or you may prefer to fill the plates in the kitchen and bring them to the table. If it's a casserole dinner, you'll probably bring the dish to the table and pass it, or serve it yourself at the hostess' place.

If you both like demitasse, get in the habit of having it regularly. Make a bit of a ceremony of serving it in the living room with your cigarettes, or at the table after dessert.

Make your party manners your everyday ones, and every day will be like a party for both of you.

Study diagram showing the placement of table appointments when the host carves and serves, page 209.

dinner for four

When you are having guests for dinner and want to simplify the serving, it's a good idea to have an accessory serving cart beside you so that you can eliminate extra trips to the kitchen. If, for instance, the salad is to be served as a separate course, it can be arranged on the top of the cart. Then, when the entreé is finished, the used dishes are put on the lower shelf of the cart, and the salad served. The dessert, also, may be served in the same manner.

We have chosen a five-course sit-down dinner to illustrate the proper way to serve. (Shown in the following diagrams.) The order may be changed, according to the number of courses served. A less formal dinner, similar to a luncheon, may consist of only two or three courses.

If the first course is to be cocktails (or juices of some sort), they should be served in the living room. The soup, or entreé in this case, is on the table when guests are seated.

If the entreé is not served individually, directly from the kitchen, the meat and vegetables are placed in front of the host ready for him to serve. The salad bowl or mold may be at the hostess' place so that she may serve the salad with the main course, if preferred.

Water glasses should be three-quarters full, and a pitcher of ice water placed on the serving cart, or somewhere within reach of the hostess.

At the end of the main course, when the table is cleared, only the water glasses, ash trays and table centerpiece are left (unless silver for the last course was placed on the table rather than brought in with the dessert and finger bowls).

When the dessert is not served from the kitchen, it may be brought in with the plates and placed before the hostess for serving.

The beverage may be served with the dessert or later in the living room. If served with the dessert, the pot, cups, saucers, creamer and sugar bowl are placed in front of either the host or hostess for serving.

A strictly formal dinner requires efficient help in both the kitchen and the dining room, and should not be attempted without it.

In this type of service, no food is served from the table. Service plates are required as a base for smaller dishes and plates containing food, as well as for added elegance of the table setting.

Plates are usually served directly from the kitchen to each guest by a waitress, serving always from the left. Or, as an

Order of Service for Five-Course Dinner

1. SEAFOOD

Place setting may look like this when guest comes to table. If seafood cocktail comes first, fork goes on right. If it's a fruit cocktail, spoon is on far right. Bread and butter plates are not used in a strictly formal dinner.

2. SOUP

If soup is served, it comes next in a soup plate. It is set on service or dinner plate after seafood is removed. Soup spoon is on right.

3. MAIN COURSE

Dinner plate is used for the main course. Dinner fork is at far left, knife at right. Wine is poured.

4. SALAD COURSE

Salad plate is used for salad course, also salad fork. After the salad course, the table is cleared. Wine glass may be removed at this time or left on, as preferred.

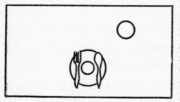

5. DESSERT COURSE

Dessert plate is set down before each place with fork and spoon on it, fork at left, spoon at right. If a finger bowl is used, it may be brought in at this time on the dessert plate with a doily underneath it. Guest removes finger bowl with doily and places it above the plate to the left and removes silver from the plate. Host or hostess may serve the dessert at the table. Coffee may be served at the table or in the living room.

alternative, the waitress may pass platters of food with individual portions to each guest so that he may help himself.

No bread-and-butter plates are used on the strictly formal dinner table. If hard rolls are served, they are supposed to be eaten without butter. Soft dinner rolls are already buttered when served.

Second helpings of food are never offered.

In formal service, there is always a plate either with or without food in front of the guest until the table is cleared for dessert.

buffet service

Buffet-style serving is the easiest form of entertaining at mealtime and is today's most popular way for accommodating both small and large groups. It offers young homemakers a glorious opportunity for bringing out the copper casseroles, stainless-steel serving dishes, and all appropriate new electrical appliances—and to adapt the menu and the service uniquely to the shining modern equipment.

The buffet table may be as dressed-up or as casual as the mood requires, wearing formal attire for a reception affair, or vivid informal colorings for an "after-the-game" occasion. A tablecloth, a center runner, or the bare, shiny table top may be used.

If your dining room is small, you may want to push the table against the wall, placing the centerpiece at the back of the table to give more serving space. When the room is large, the table in the center is best, where guests can move around it to serve themselves, and more can be accommodated at one time. A supplementary table, serving cart or sideboard can help take the load off the main table by being attractively set up with the coffee service, dessert, and water service.

the table arrangement

There is no set formula for arranging a buffet table, but it should present an attractive, uncluttered appearance, and it should offer a convenient arrangement of food and service.

Group together the units that go well together and try to avoid a spotty effect by balancing tall items on each side of

Typical Buffet Service

the table. An arrangement of candles and flowers placed at one end of the table might be offset with a tiered compote at the other end, for example.

In line-up, the stacked plates, silver and napkins should come first, then the meat dish, hot foods and the buttered rolls last. Menus that do not require the use of a knife are recommended. The flat silver should be placed in a simple row, rather than in a fanciful pattern. The necessary serving spoons should be arranged with each dish. The napkins may be placed between the plates as they are stacked, or arranged neatly near the plates. If there is a salad, when most of the other dishes are hot, separate salad plates should be provided. Bread and rolls should be spread with butter before being served.

ways of service

The most convenient arrangement is to let guests serve themselves, then be seated at card tables which have been set up in harmony with the buffet table. This eliminates the need for silver, napkins and glassware on the buffet table. If it's a three course dinner, the first course should be at the individual places on the small tables when dinner is announced. Guests then help themselves to the main dinner course on the buffet table, while their first-course dishes are being removed from the small tables. This type of semi-self-service usually requires a maid (or some helpful someone) to be in attendance, so that the hostess (and the host also if needed) may remain at the buffet table to help serve the guests in line.

If your kitchen is especially attractive it's a novel idea to

Sideboard Buffet Service

Double-Line Buffet

with card table seating

let your guests help themselves to hot foods right off the top of the stove, after picking up their trays and plates from the dining-room table. Or, if you are blessed with electric skillets and casseroles, or candle-warmed receptacles, keep the hot foods hot right on the buffet itself.

The dessert course is customarily served directly from the kitchen at a buffet supper. Or the guests may remove their own used plates, if the hostess has planned it that way, then help themselves to dessert and beverage from a teacart or side table.

If small tables cannot be provided for guests, see to it that each guest has a tray on which to balance his plate, silver and coffee cup. Men don't mind the tray idea, usually, but they do balk at juggling their suppers in multiple units on their laps.

For picnic suppers, you may want to use the individual trays which are made with divided cardboard liners that can be thrown away after use. This sort of service eliminates dishwashing and is a great convenience to the hostess, but is not recommended for serving hot foods or for any but the most informal outdoor affairs.

See diagrams for service ideas to make your entertaining easier.

informal tea service

Afternoon tea, served in your living room to a small group of friends, should be served from a large tray placed on a table in front of the hostess. The table should be high enough for one's knees to fit under it, as a low table places the hostess in an awkward and uncomfortable position.

A card table or a folding tray table will serve very well when covered with a pretty tea cloth (about forty-five inches square, as described in the chapter on linens). Or you may use a circular table top on your bridge table, covering it with an attractive round tea cloth reaching almost to the floor. For a less elaborate spot of tea, it is simple enough to place the tea tray on your bare-topped coffee table, if it is large enough and not too low for convenient serving.

The tea set (either silver or china) is arranged neatly on the tray (see diagram) and placed on the table, before the guests arrive. A teapot, a strainer, sugar and creamer are the important serving pieces, and when the tea is to steep in a china pot, a tea cosy is nice for keeping it warm. If it is a silver tea set, you will probably have a hot-water kettle with an alcohol lamp beneath it, and a waste bowl for used tea leaves.

On the tray also you'll place the tea napkins, the cups and saucers of your most delicate china, gleaming teaspoons and slices of lemon on a small plate. The cups and saucers should be individually arranged, if there is room, with a spoon placed in each saucer just under the cup handle to the right. If tray space does not permit, you may stack the cups and saucers in twos with the handles turned toward the hostess.

Since tea food usually consists only of light finger food, the preferred service is to have the cup in its saucer rather than resting on a tea plate. The depression in the saucer keeps the cup steady and gives a more graceful appearance to the ensemble.

If more food is to be served than can be accommodated on a saucer, you may also have a stack of little tea plates on the tray, with separate napkins between each plate or beside them. Each plate is lifted off with its own napkin, and served after the filled teacups and saucers have been passed. Small forks for pastries and small knives for spreading jams or cheese should be placed on the individual plates before they are passed.

Plates of thin sandwiches, small cakes or cookies, salted nuts, candied fruit or other confections may be placed around the tea tray, or they may be on a near-by table or muffin stand, ready to be passed.

formal tea service

Tea for a number of people should be served from the dining-room table or from a large table placed at the end of the living room. At a big party there might be a table at each end of the room—one for serving tea and the other for serving coffee.

Special friends should be asked to pour—one to preside over the tea service at one end of the table (when there is one main table), and another to serve coffee at the other end. In warm weather a light punch may be served instead of one of the beverages mentioned if you prefer. Several people should be scheduled to pour if the party is fairly large, so that no one is confined to the table for longer than fifteen or twenty minutes.

Decorative effects may be elaborate for a tea table with candles and flower arrangements standing high, since guests are

Formal Tea Service

Informal Tea Service

not seated at the table. (See page 221 for arrangement of tea table.)

cocktail party setup

Cocktail parties in small quarters call for getting geared up right to mix and serve drinks both from the kitchen and from the living room, according to your needs.

Besides the proper glasses, specified in Chapter IV, you'll need certain other items of equipment for good bartending.

The list should include:

a jigger measure

a bottle opener (the hook variety)

a beer-can opener

a good corkscrew

a paring knife for cutting lemon peel

a long bar spoon for measuring sugar, etc. and for stirring cocktails

a good stopper for soda bottles

a muddler for mashing sugar and bitters

an ice pick or patented ice shaver

a vacuum ice bucket

a wooden mallet for crushing ice

a cocktail shaker (of metal or glass, with a good screw top and easy pouring spout)

a lemon squeezer

a tall mixing glass or pitcher for making Martinis and Manhattans (the mixing glass requires a circular wire strainer for pouring)

Late Evening Snack Table

Cocktail Tray Arrangement

a number of trays—one oversized, several small trays for
passing drinks and collecting empties
an electric blender comes in handy for mixing frappés and
flips

When you are having a big cocktail party, it's wise to set up
bar on the dining-room table or on a large gate-leg table at the
end of the living room. To protect the top of the furniture
cover it with a sheet of plastic or colorful plastic mats.

For smaller parties, you may use a portable cart which can
be moved to the most convenient place in the room. Or you
might set up a tray and place it on a sturdy table in the living
room, where guests can mix their own drinks after the host
has served the first round.

Staples which should be placed on the cocktail tray include Angostura bitters, orange bitters, club soda water, pitcher of plain water, ginger ale, cocktail olives, cocktail onions,
maraschino cherries, lemons and sugar. Be sure to provide
soft drinks such as tomato juice, cola, etc., for nondrinkers at
your parties.

Study the diagrams to help you get organized for the kind
of occasion you are planning.

Tips for Host and Hostess

As soon as you are settled in your new home, your first
thoughts will turn to entertaining your family and friends.
You want these first parties to be a huge success, and, while
you may have entertained at home under the tutelage of your
mother, you still may feel a little unsure of yourself—so here
are some pointers to help you get organized for your parties.

1. The first ingredient for a successful party is your own (and your husband's) sincere desire to have your friends in your new home. When guests feel your warmth and hospitality, they catch the contagion of it and are sure to enjoy themselves. Most of all, be sure you two have fun at your own parties, and make the most of the talents you have for hosting and hostessing. Remember that your chief interest should not be just in following convention, but always in doing the gracious and considerate thing.

2. Next, it is the preparation which is really the backbone of a good party. This doesn't necessarily mean just the day-before preparations.

> *It means* devising a method of serving food and liquor that is convenient for you and comfortable for your guests. Don't be afraid to set your own rules if the service or circumstances can be bettered, but don't break a rule merely through ignorance.

> *It means* setting up an orderly kitchen where you can find things readily, so that even an impromptu party can be carried off with grace.

> *It means* preparedness from the food standpoint. Have an emergency shelf for party food, suitable to both dinner and snack fare. Have several quick menus tacked to the shelf in readiness. If you have a freezer compartment in the refrigerator, keep *extras* on hand there, too.

3. Consider your budget at all times. Formal entertaining requires a pretty big budget and really perfect service. So plan small parties at first. Invite couples who are congenial and have interests in common. If you are entertaining more

than four for dinner and are maidless, make it a rule to serve buffet sit-down style, that is, with each one serving his own plate, but having *all* sit down at tables to enjoy the food.

4. Plan your menus together, the two of you, and have a sort of dress rehearsal of the party. Check supplies, the necessary equipment for cocktails, dinner, etc., the serving dishes and spoons needed for everything you are serving.

Keep it all within the limit of your pocketbook and your energies, and you can't help but have a happy time.

what type parties for you?

The three basic types of parties are the cocktail party, the seated dinner party and the buffet supper.

All others are variations of these. When you have mastered the techniques of these three, you should be able to cope with any type of party your budget will allow.

if it's a cocktail party

Try to invite a group of people who will enjoy getting to know one another, not just a group who happen to be your friends.

Invite them to cocktails for a definite time—say, five to seven or six to eight—but be prepared to have them overstay the specified time from at least a half hour to an hour.

If your choice of drinks is limited, mention what you have and let each guest make his choice. If you are about to mix drinks before dinner for a small group, you might suggest a couple of your cocktail specialties and take a poll on preferences.

Cocktail ingredients must be of the best quality available to be worthy of the drink. Be sure of your formulae for making them, then try them out carefully beforehand to smooth out any of the faults. When you have the technique mastered, adhere to the same measurements and standards every time you make your specialties.

When giving a large cocktail party, the host should mix the cocktails just before the party starts and store them in the refrigerator. With an electric blender it's quite simple to mix certain types of drinks on short order, but unless there is someone tending the bar during the party, it's best to have a large quantity of mixture all ready to serve.

For a crowd trays of cocktails should be passed, and long drinks also should be available. Be mindful of the season of the year. In summertime, be prepared to favor the tall Collins.

It's a mark of the connoisseur to have chilled glasses, not only for the cocktails, but for the highballs you serve as well. The charged water or ginger ale which goes into their making also should be chilled in advance.

Keep the canapés simple unless you have extra help. Fancy crackers, popcorn, nuts, a sharp cheese, or a tasty dip that can be made ahead of time are good choices. It is difficult to serve hot hors d'oeuvres unless you bring your electric grill right into the living room and set it up on a serving table with someone stationed to attend to it constantly. Sweets are never served with cocktails or highballs.

if it's a dinner party or buffet

Besides an attractive table, the foundation of a dinner party is good food, good drink and good conversation.

Serve a meal that you do well. Don't experiment on your guests. Try to develop a few specialties for parties that you know are infallible. Current newspapers and magazines are filled with exciting recipes that have been tested by experts and should be reliable enough for you to try out on your hubby before company comes. Try not to select dishes that would be ruined if the cocktail hour lasts longer than you planned.

Establish the habit of being on time in serving your party meals. When you invite guests for cocktails at 6:30 and dinner at 7:00, adhere to it as strictly as possible. Your reputation for orderliness and graciousness as a hostess will be marked early in your career if you set your standards and live by them.

Allow a half hour for serving cocktails and fifteen minutes more for late arrivals, then start serving dinner, even though there may be a stray guest who hasn't yet arrived. Dinner shouldn't be spoiled for many people while waiting for one or two late arrivals.

Take advantage of dishes that can be prepared ahead of time or that require a minimum of your attention after the guests arrive, so that you can enjoy the cocktail hour with them.

If it's a sit-down dinner, don't invite more guests than you can serve conveniently.

Place cards are not necessary unless you are having such a

crowd that it would be unwieldy to tell each guest where he is to sit when you assemble around the table.

The serving of nuts and candies at dinner parties is considered by many a bit old-fashioned today. But if you do wish to serve them as a final fillip to the meal, guard against too many small dishes giving your table a cluttered look.

For a buffet, provide food that is easy to eat from a tray, or from a small table. The little fold-away tables that can be tucked in a closet until partytime arrives are perfect for buffet parties. (See buffet service suggestions, page 213, for other ideas.)

Don't plan elaborate dishes if you don't have much time for advance preparation. Many foods that are suitable for buffet may be cooked the night before, cooled and refrigerated. They often taste even better after reheating.

Appoint some of your guests to help serve if it simplifies things for you. If your kitchen is tiny, they may only add to the confusion there, but can aid you best by carrying out duties elsewhere.

Reputations are often built on the important *little* things. Make your first claim to fame the art of making a whooping good cup of coffee. Since it's usually the last flavor to be recorded at a dinner party, let the memory that lingers on be an unforgettably pleasant one.

ACKNOWLEDGMENT

The authors wish to thank the following manufacturers who so kindly supplied us with background material for use in this book: Towle Silversmiths, International Silver Co., Reed & Barton Silversmiths, Oneida, Ltd., Lunt Silversmiths, The Gorham Company, The Sterling Silversmiths Guild of America, Josiah Wedgwood & Sons, Ltd., Lenox, Inc., Stangl Pottery, Midhurst China Corp., Rosenthal-Block China Co., Syracuse China Corp., Pickard Inc., Haviland & Co., Flintridge China Co., Gladding McBean Co., Fostoria Glass Co., The Cambridge Glass Co., Cannon Mills, Fieldcrest Mills, Wamsutta Mills, General Electric Co., Sunbeam Corp., Landers, Frary & Clark, and Hamilton Beach Co.

We are especially grateful for specific information received from James B. McCutcheon's on trousseau linens; to Herman W. Graef, Kitchen Planning Consultant, Cox Kitchens, and Lewis & Conger regarding kitchen planning designs; and to Betsy Abbott, Wedding Gift Counselor of B. Altman & Co., for wedding-gift data. For research material supplied by the Better Buymanship series from Household Finance Corp., we also wish to express appreciation.

INDEX

INDEX

Aluminum kitchenware, 117-180
American Colonial silver, 45-46
American glass, 67-69
American silver, 42-43
Appliances
    automatic electric irons, 164-166
    blenders, 144-148, 171
    care of, 170
    coffeemakers, 139-141, 172
    combination grill and waffle iron, 150-153, 172
    deep-fat fryers, 159-161
    electric broilers, 153-155, 171
    electric knife sharpeners, 163-164
    electric roasters, 157-159
    electric skillets, 161-163
    mixers, 141-144
    nonautomatic electric irons, 166-167
    rotisserie broilers, 155-157, 172
    rules for buying, 135-136
    steam irons, 167-170, 172
    suggestions for selection, 170-173
    toasters, 136-138, 171, 172
    waffle irons, 148-150
Atmosphere of your home, 16-17
Attitude toward homemaking, 17-18

Bathroom linens
    amount to buy, 132
    care of, 132-133
    color in towels, 128

Bathroom linens—*cont.*
    monograms, 130
    shopping for towels, 127-128
    sizes of towels, 129
    small towels, 129-130
    variations of towels, 126-127
Bedroom linens
    blanket covers, 121
    blankets, 116-118
    bedspreads, 121-122
    breaking strength of sheets, 109
    care of blankets, 120-121
    care of sheets, 114-115
    comforters, 122, 124
    electric blankets and sheets, 119-120
    grades of cotton in sheets, 109-110
    history of towels, 124-126
    mattress covers, 115-116
    monograms, 113
    number of sheets to buy, 114
    pillows and pillowcases, 112, 114
    rules for buying sheets and pillowcases, 107-115
    selvage of sheets, 110
    sheet and pillowcase sizes, 110-111, 123
    shopping for blankets, 118-119, 123
    sizing, 109
    summary of needs, 124
    thread count of sheets, 108-109
    types of sheeting, 107-108
    weight of sheets, 109

233